LAMPWORKS
FULL-SIZE PATTERNS FOR STAINED GLASS LAMPSHADES

10" Diameter

CHARLES KNAPP

21" Diameter

BRIAN EAGLE

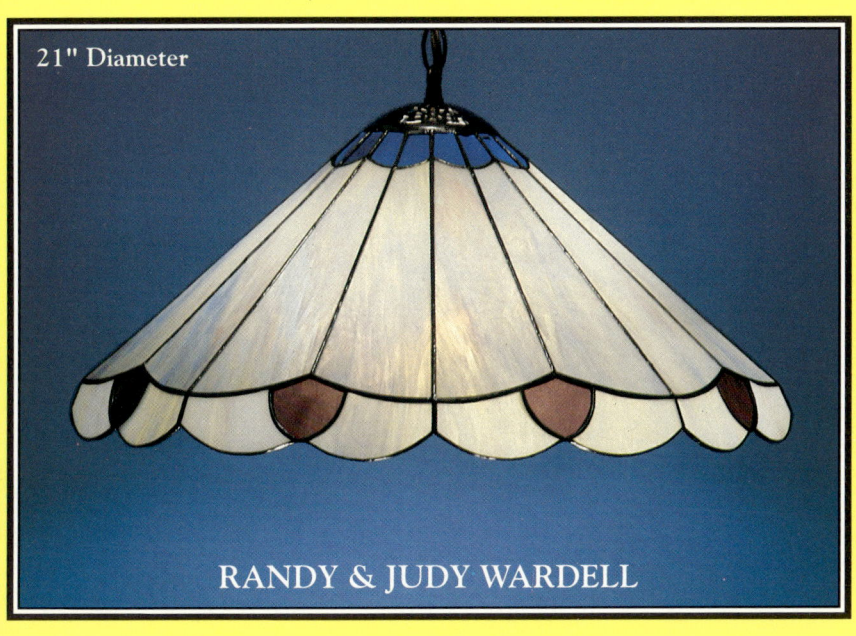

21" Diameter

RANDY & JUDY WARDELL

15" Diameter

BRIAN EAGLE

LAMPWORKS
FULL-SIZE PATTERNS FOR STAINED GLASS LAMPSHADES

12" Diameter

LINDA HOLMES

16 1/2" Diameter

CHARLES KNAPP

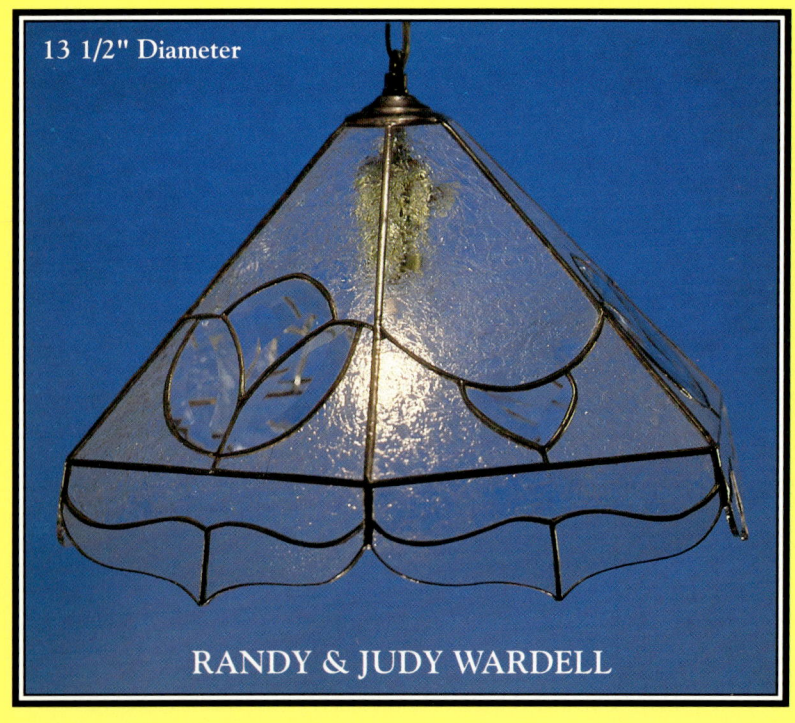

13 1/2" Diameter

RANDY & JUDY WARDELL

15 1/2" Diameter

LINDA HOLMES

LAMPWORKS
FULL-SIZE PATTERNS FOR STAINED GLASS LAMPSHADES

Designs by:

Brian Eagle
Linda Holmes
Charles Knapp
Randy & Judy Wardell

Typesetting and Layout
Atelier Typographic

Photography
Randy & Judy Wardell

Printed in Canada
by
Thorn Press

Special Thanks
Richard Bond
Stephan Gray
Barb Pickthorne
Ed Saikaley

Wardell
PUBLICATIONS

P.O. Box 1501, Belleville, Ontario, Canada K8N 5J2

A NOTE FROM THE PUBLISHER

Lampworks is the fourth in a series of lampshade pattern books from Wardell Publications. It is a collection of original works from five designers.

- Randy and Judy Wardell are authors and publishers of a variety of books for the stained glass craft.
- Charles Knapp is the author of a Wardell book titled "Designs for Lamps" and has produced an instructional video tape on lampshade assembly.
- Linda Holmes is an independent artist who designs and constructs various projects for her clients.
- Brian Eagle is co-owner of a full service studio where he teaches stained glass and sells his popular lampshades.

These five authors bring their unique designing skills to this book and have provided a wide selection of styles and sizes to satisfy many applications. These lamps, as in all Wardell Publication books, do not require an expensive mold or form to construct. They are assembled using a flat foil technique which is explained through the use of photographs and a special instruction guide.

Lampshades are one of the most popular projects for stained glass crafters. Regardless of your skill level or application, you are sure to find a suitable project in this book.

Special Studio Recognition to:

Brian Eagle — Ottawa, Ontario, Canada

Huntsville, Ontario, Canada

Copyright © 1988 by
Randy & Judy Wardell
Wardell Ventures Ltd.

ALL RIGHTS RESERVED. No part of this book may be reproduced for any reason (except to construct one of the projects) or by any means including photocopying, electronic, mechanical or otherwise, without permission in writing from the copyright owners.

Canadian Cataloguing in Publication Data

Main entry under title:

Lampworks : full-size patterns for stained glass lampshades

ISBN 0-919985-14-9

1. Lampshades, Glass- Patterns.
2. Glass painting and staining - Patterns
I. Eagle, Brian, 1953-

NK5440.L3L35 1988   749'.63   C88-093724-6

CONTENTS

	PAGE
Constructing A Copper Foil Lampshade	
Step by Step Instruction	7-11
Alternate Lamp Assembly Method	10
Joiner Pieces	11
Hanging Hardware	
Inverted Lamp Installation	11
Spider	12
Vase Cap	13
Finishing Your Project	
Wire Reinforcement	14
Cleaning	14
Patina	14
Photocopying Your Pattern	14

FULL-SIZE LAMPSHADE PATTERNS

PROJECT #	LAMPSHADE	INFORMATION PAGE	PATTERN PAGE
1. RIBBON'S II		15	16
2. ELEGANCE		15	17
3. COUNTRY DOME		18	19
4. PRESTIGE		18	20 & 21
5. SWEET DREAMS		22	23
6. MALLARD DUCK		22	24 & 25

FULL-SIZE LAMPSHADE PATTERNS

PROJECT #	LAMPSHADE	INFORMATION PAGE	PATTERN PAGE
7.	THERESA'S FLOWER	26	27
8.	BEVEL BELTED CONE	26	28 & 29
9.	NOUVEAU CLASSIC	30	30 & 31
10.	BARCELONA CONE	32	38, 40
11.	OVERHEAD BLOOM	32	39
12.	DRAPERY	33	41, 43
13.	LILY	33	42
14.	TULIP BELL	34	44, 46
15.	RIDEAU	34	45
16.	OLD ROSE	35	35, 36 & 37

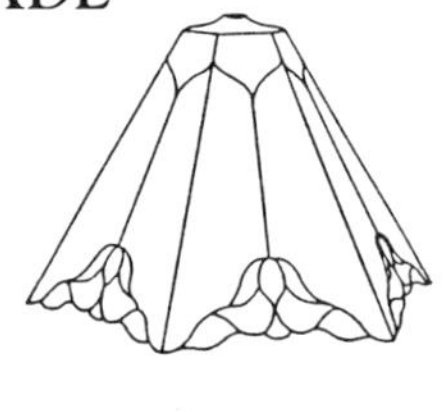

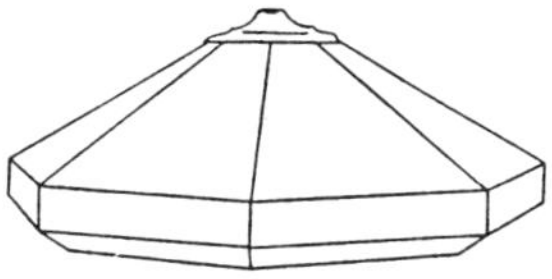

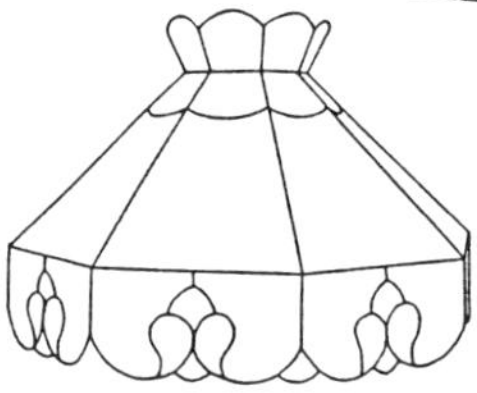

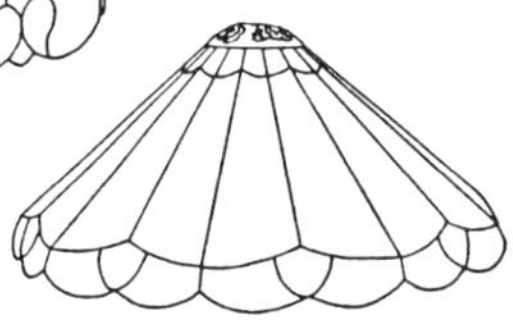

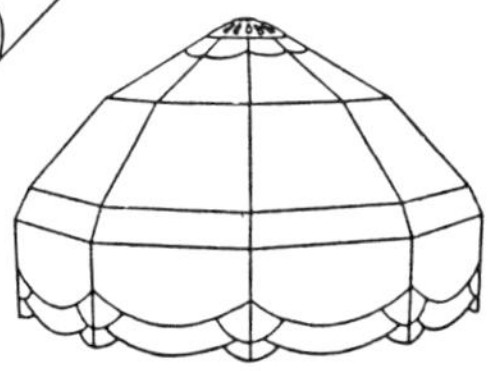

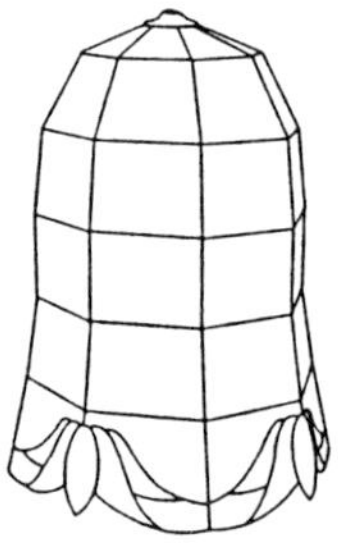

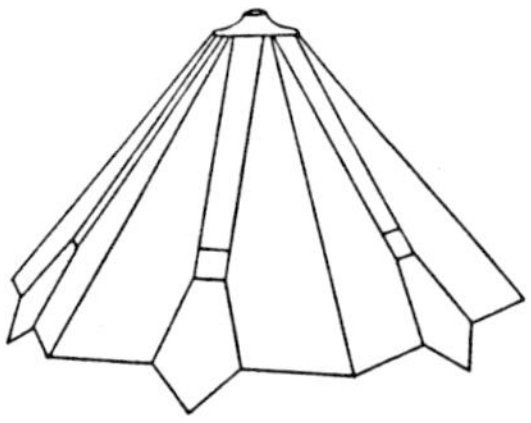

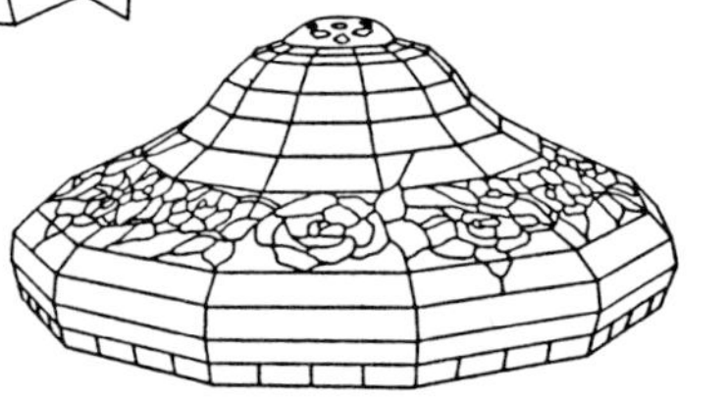

CONSTRUCTING A FOILED LAMPSHADE

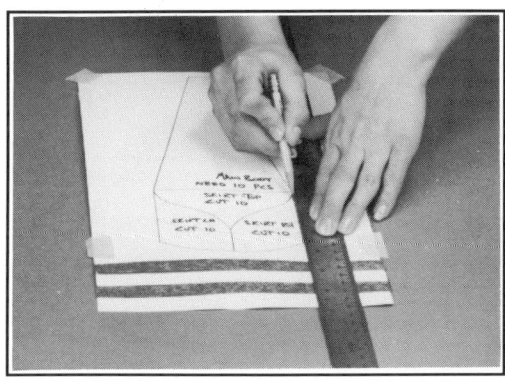

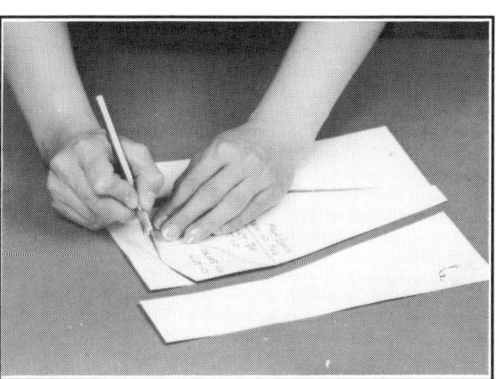

Step 1: Trace the pattern, making two copies, one on standard paper and one on card stock paper.

First — Cut completely around the perimeter (outside) lines of the lamp pattern, following the center of each line.

Second — Cut the interior design line following the center of each line. This will align each section to match the pattern above and below it.

Step 2: Carefully trace the pattern onto the glass using a felt-tip pen and cut the glass piece by scoring on the inside of the marker line. *You must always cut the line away* so the marker line is on the waste glass when you break it off. Check your glass piece with the pattern to verify that they are exactly the same size and shape. If the glass is not exact, you must grind it or cut it. Adjust your scoring to be more precise when scoring the next piece. Continue cutting your glass until all pieces are complete.

NOTE: When a pattern calls for Cut 1 Up 1 Down, you are required to trace and cut the glass with pattern facing you, **OVERTURN** pattern and trace and cut the glass with pattern facing down.

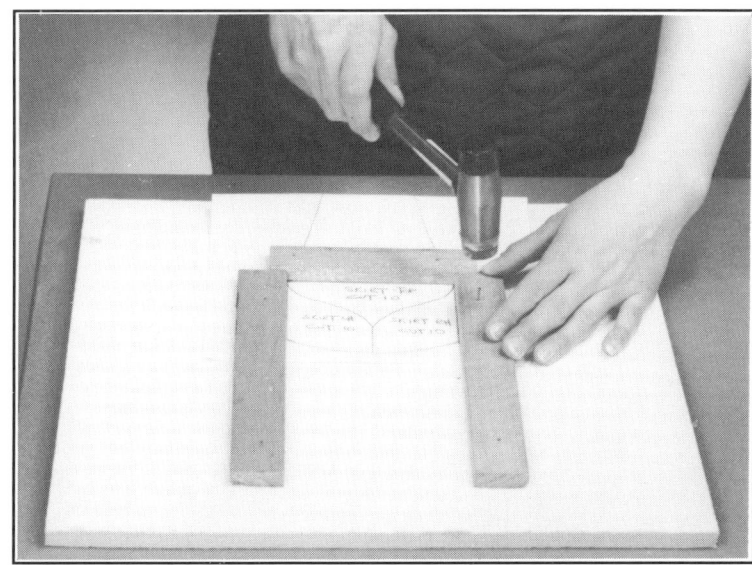

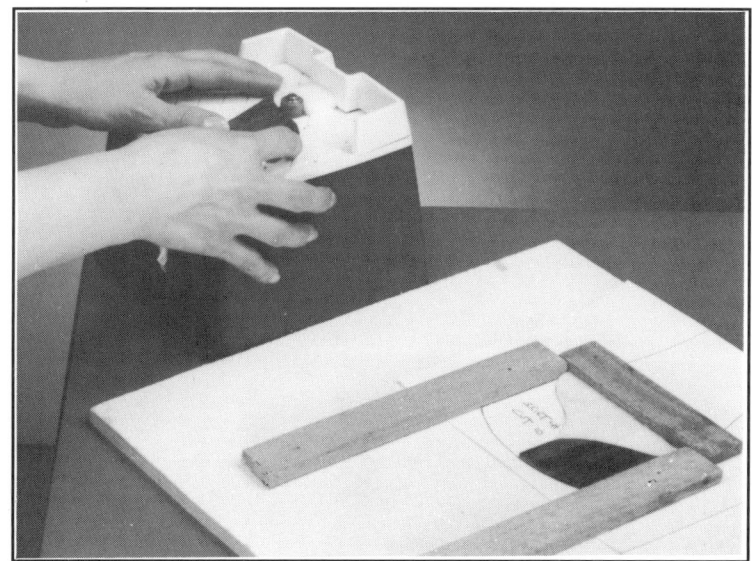

Step 3: When constructing a lamp that has panels with interior designs (a flat section containing two or more pieces), they must be fitted and assembled in a jig. Lay the working drawing (paper copy) of the pattern on your work table, face up. Nail three pieces of glazing lath onto your drawing so the outside line of the section to be assembled is half showing.

Step 4: Place one set of glass pieces into the jig as your drawing shows. If the pieces do not fit accurately, you will have to groze or grind them to fit or cut new ones. When the pieces fit into the jig correctly, clean each piece of glass and copper foil it.

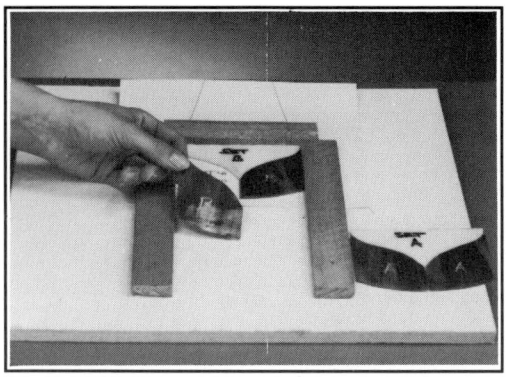

NOTE: If you intend to grind and fit all panel sets before foiling and assembling, you must code each set before removing them from the jig and keep the matched sets together.

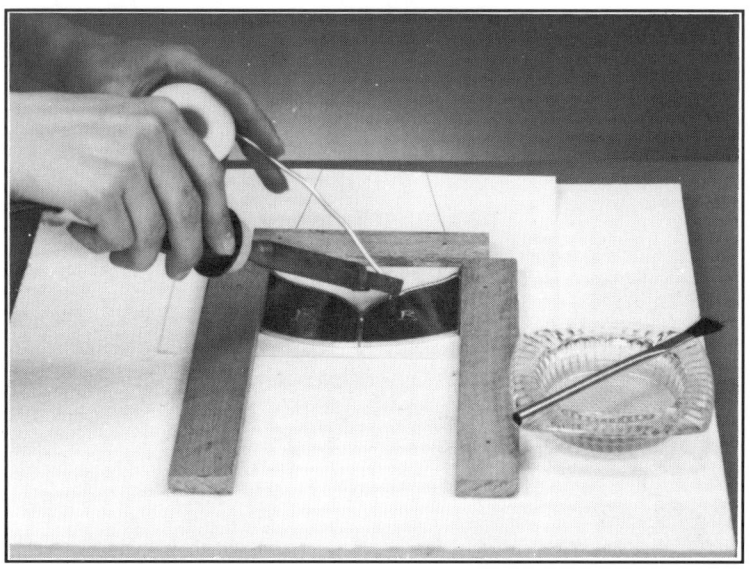

Step 5: Place the foiled glass pieces back into the jig and flat solder them. Remove the panel from the jig, turn it over and flat solder the other side. Finish by running a solder bead on the face side. Repeat for all panels.

Step 6: Start the lamp assembly with the row that is called the main body. This is the large section closest to the vase cap opening. Lay these pieces face side up on the work bench in a semi-circle. Use black plastic electrical tape (or in a pinch, masking tape) and tape the sections together. The areas where tape will come in contact with the glass *must be* clean or the tape will not adhere.

Step 7: Carefully raise this row up into a cone shape, keeping the large diameter end on the bench. Bring the two adjoining side sections together and tape.

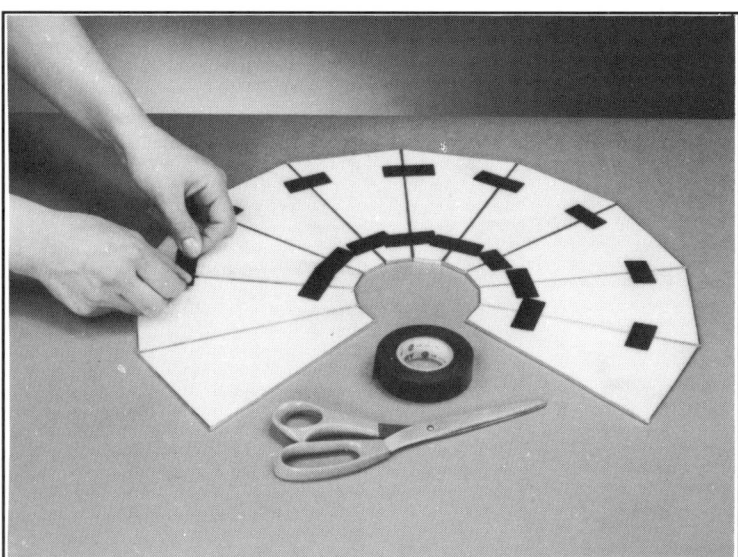

EXCEPTION: When constructing a lamp which has several rows that make up the main body (eg. dome style lamp), the top row is often at a very flat angle which makes it difficult to raise into a cone shape. In a case such as this choose a row with a greater angle (perhaps the second row) as the start row and proceed as above. Be sure to add the top row and vase cap next for greater strength.

Step 8: You must be sure the bottom of the cone is *flat* on the bench. Flux and tack solder each seam at the bottom corner by applying a small dab of molten solder with the tip of your iron.

Step 9: Flux and solder completely around the top opening. Flat solder down the outside of each seam as best you can (leaving tape on) to strengthen the assembly.

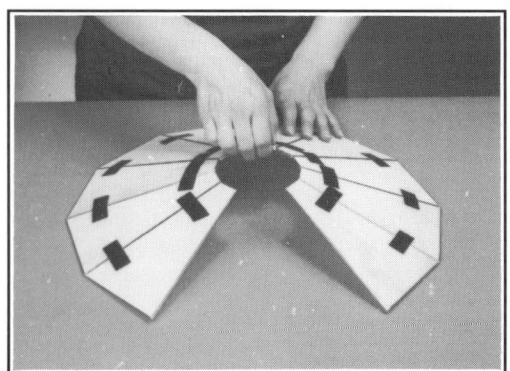
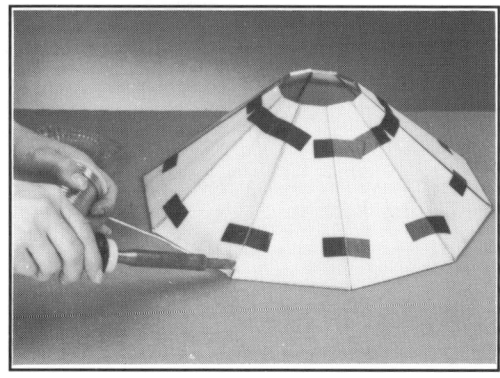
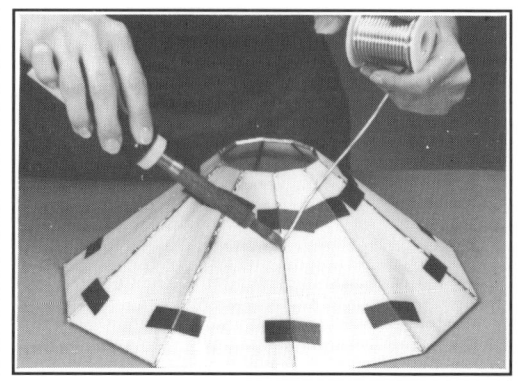

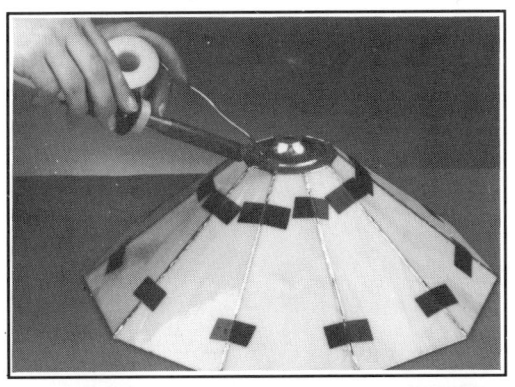

Step 10 : You have probably noticed how flimsy the lamp is at this stage. Attach the vase cap or spider now to strengthen its form (see Page 12 &13). The bottom must be sitting flat on the table when installing the vase cap to ensure the lamp has a proper shape. When the cap is soldered securely to the outside, carefully turn the lamp over and solder all inside seams and around the vase cap.

Step 11: Place your lamp upside down into a soldering box. (A cardboard box with newspapers loosely crumpled inside.) The assembly will continue by adding the panels of the next row (in the example shown it is the skirt or bottom row). Position and tack solder the first panel of this row to the main body.

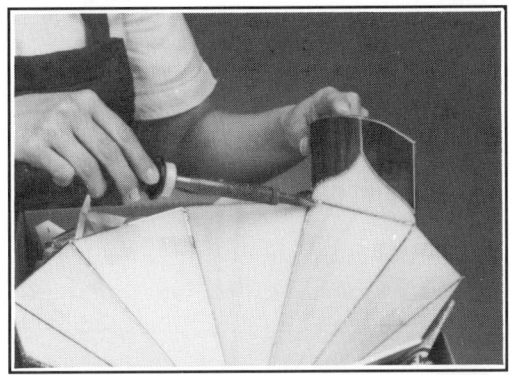

Step 12: Place the second panel beside the first and tack it to the main body. Position pieces one and two until the seam meets evenly and tack solder together.

Step 13: Continue by adding the remaining panels in order around the lamp, tacking one to the other as you go. When the complete row is assembled, flat solder all the inside seams before moving on. Continue to add rows (if necessary) until the lower lamp is complete. Finish by soldering completely around the bottom edge for more strength and stability.

Step 14: Turn the lamp right side up in the soldering box. If you are constructing a lamp with a crown (upper most row) use the same procedure as described for the skirt assembly in Step 11, 12 & 13.

Step 15: The lamp should be completely assembled now and ready for final soldering. Remove all remaining tape. Position the lamp in the soldering box and level the seam you intend to solder (horizontal to the floor). Take your time and run a bead of solder. If the molten solder is flowing away from the seam or appears to be running downhill, this indicates the seam is not perfectly level. Reposition the lamp in the box and resume soldering.

HINT: If you are trying to fill a gap (a space between two foiled pieces), and the molten solder falls through, cover the space from the inside with masking tape to keep the solder from dripping.

Step 16: When you have completed soldering, do a quality check of all seams inside and out to make sure they are finished and uniform. Fine bead soldering is a difficult skill to master, don't be discouraged, remember practice makes perfect.

To finish your lamp, solder a wire around the bottom edge. For instruction and details see Page 14.
To clean your project of flux and solder residue use a glass cleaner, see Page 14.
To apply antique patina to the solder beads (a coppery or black color), see Page 14.

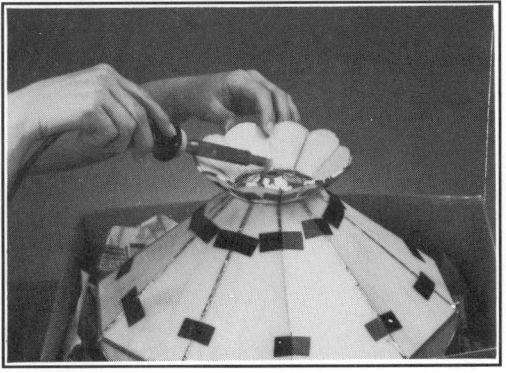
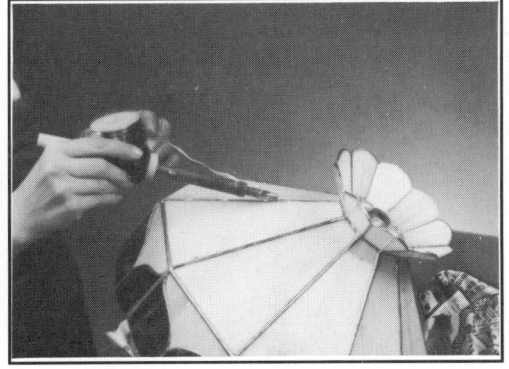
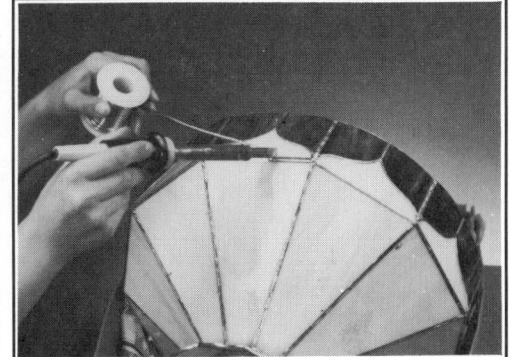

ALTERNATE LAMP ASSEMBLY METHOD

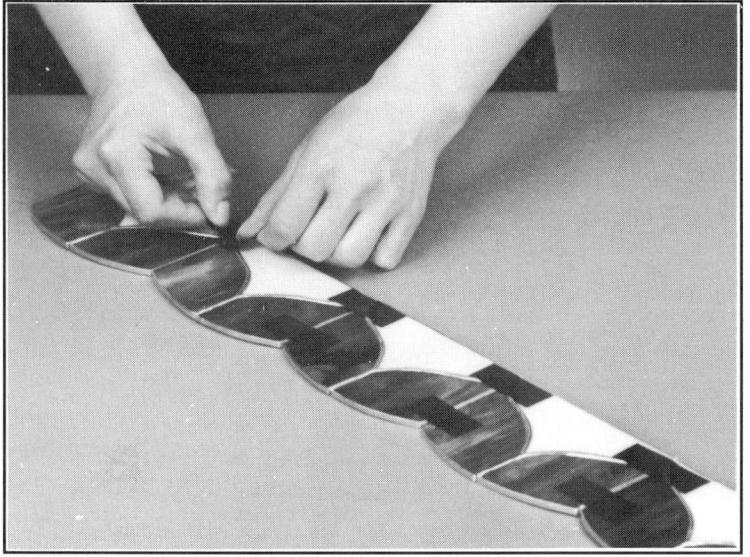

Instead of the row assembly described earlier, an alternative used by many crafters is a system called row-on-row assembly. To use this method, substitute steps 11, 12, 13 & 14 in lamp assembly description.

Step 11: Place your lamp upside down into a soldering box. (A cardboard box with newspapers loosely crumpled inside as shown.) The assembly will continue by adding the panels of the next row (in the example shown it is the skirt or bottom row). Lay these panels in sequence, side by side and face up on your bench.

EXCEPTION: As the angle of the sections increase, as happens in very small lamps or lamps with only 6 or 8 sides, the tape can become very tight and may not stretch sufficiently. Try putting the tape on the back-side instead of the face-side.

Tape them together in the same manner as you taped the main body. Gently lift the row on its edge, bend it around into a circle and tape the ends together. Tack solder all seams at top and bottom corners only.

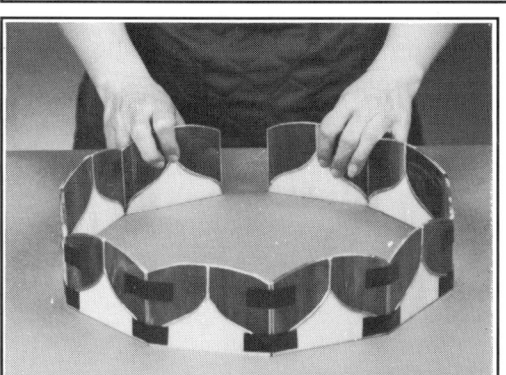

Step 12: Your main body section should be upside down in the soldering box. Gently lift the skirt and place it on the main body. The seam corners of the two sections must line up one to the other. Tack solder the sections together at these corners.

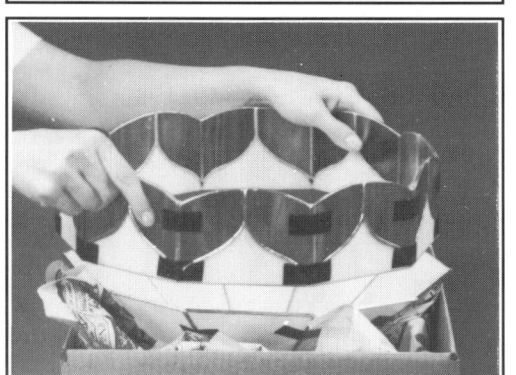

Step 13: When the complete row is attached, flat solder all the inside seams for more strength and stability before moving on.

Step 14: Turn the lamp right side up in the soldering box. If you are constructing a lamp with a crown (upper most row) use the same procedure as for the skirt assembly in Steps 11, 12 & 13.

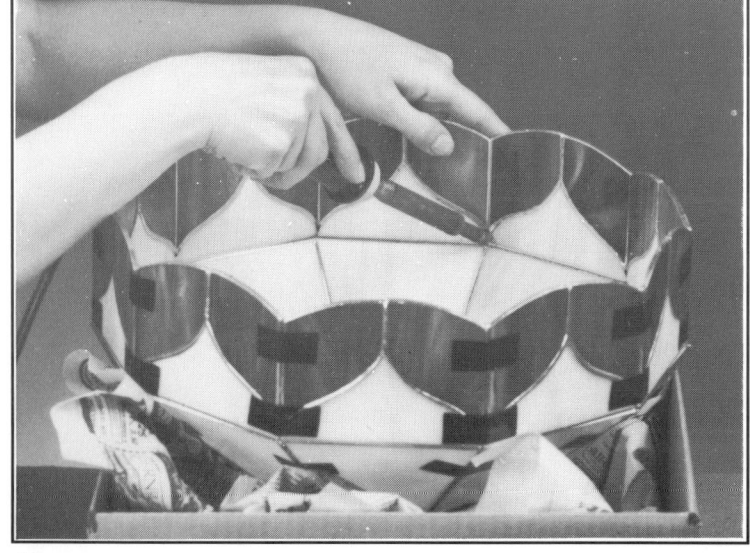
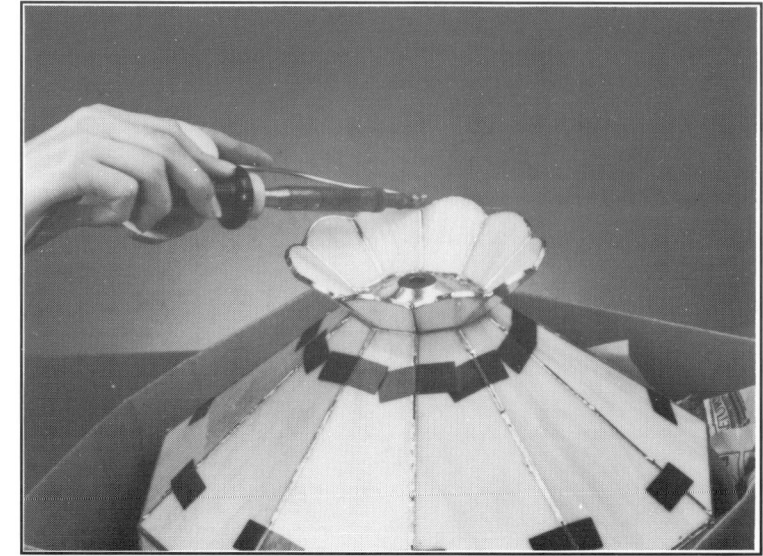

JOINER PIECES

Some lampshades must have glass (joiner) pieces inserted to join the sections once the shade has been assembled. A joiner piece usually bridges a gap between two sections which are attached at an angle to one another.

Step 1. Place the pattern for the joiner piece in the appropriate space to see if the size is satisfactory. If the pattern correctly fits the space, cut out the glass piece. In most cases the pattern will not fit well. This is due to inevitable variations in glass cutting and assembly angle.

Step 2. If the pattern fit is unacceptable you must make a new pattern of the space by placing a piece of pattern card underneath the hole and tracing around it with a marking pen. Cut the glass for the joiner piece according to this new pattern.

NOTE: Verify the size of each space individually with the pattern before cutting the glass.

 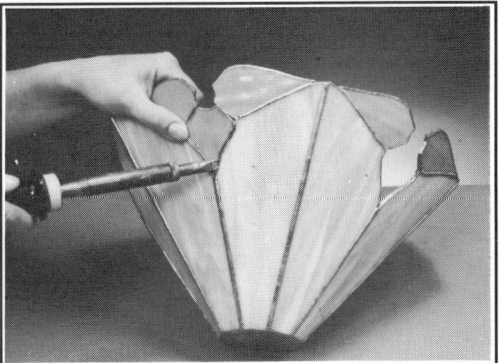 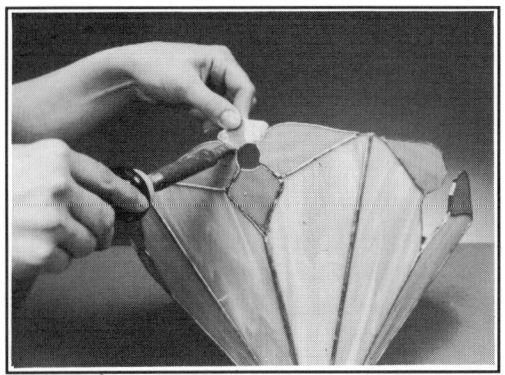

Step 3. Fit the glass piece into its designated space by grinding or grozing as necessary. Wrap the piece with copper foil. Insert it into the space so the edges are flush with the adjacent sections and tack solder it. Do not be too concerned if all edges are not completely flush since that is virtually impossible.

Step 4. Verify the pattern for the next joiner piece and cut the glass piece. Wrap it with copper foil, insert into place and tack solder it. Repeat this procedure for each joiner piece until all are installed. Finish the seams with a solder bead.

INVERTED LAMP INSTALLATION

WARNING: When wiring and installing your lamp you must consider all federal and local electrical codes and regulations.

The most common method of installing an inverted shade is by using a standard 2 or 3 way bulb fixture. Often you will find this type of fixture already installed in your home. It consists of a canopy, the bulb fixture, a threaded nipple extender and a lock nut & finial (see drawing). The fixture is hard wired (permanently) to the ceiling electrical box (see warning above) and the inverted stained glass lampshade is attached to the nipple, between the locknut and the finial. You must adjust the length of the nipple according to the depth of the shade (a deeper shade will require a longer nipple). When choosing a bulb fixture, be sure to obtain one with riveted brackets. This will ensure proper strength to support heavy glass shades.

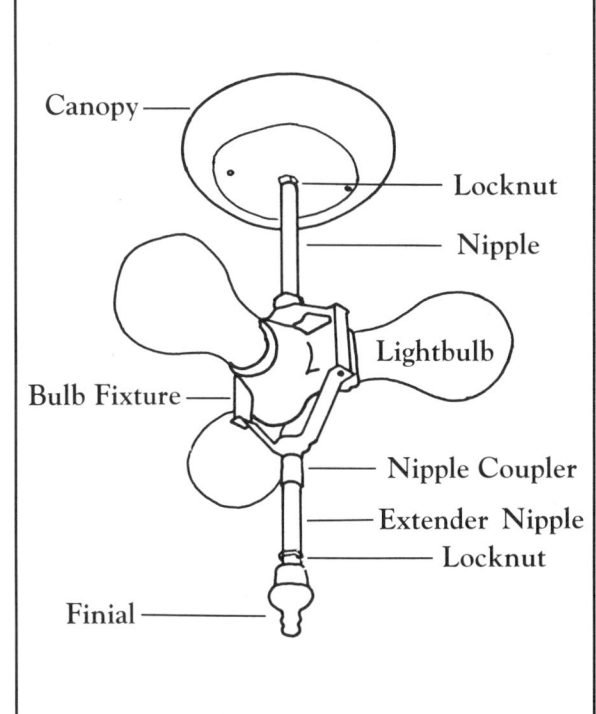

11

FINISHING YOUR PROJECT

HANGING HARDWARE

1. Lamp Hanging Hardware: This is an integral part of a lampshade. It must be securely soldered to the top opening of a lampshade to solidify the structure and to provide hanging support for the electrical hardware. There are many different types of hanging hardware available, we will describe the two most common:

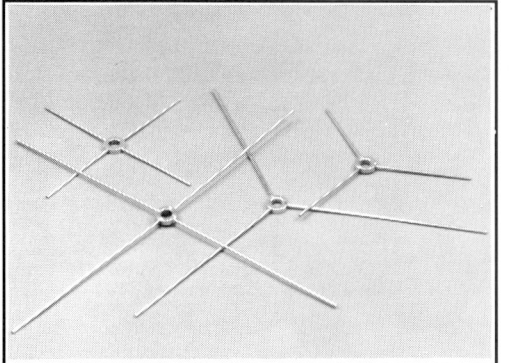

SPIDER

This is a brass ring about one inch in diameter with 3 or 4 arms radiating out from 6" to 12". The number of arms must divide evenly into the number of sides of your shade. For example, a six-sided shade requires a 3 arm spider while an eight-sided shade requires a 4 arm spider.

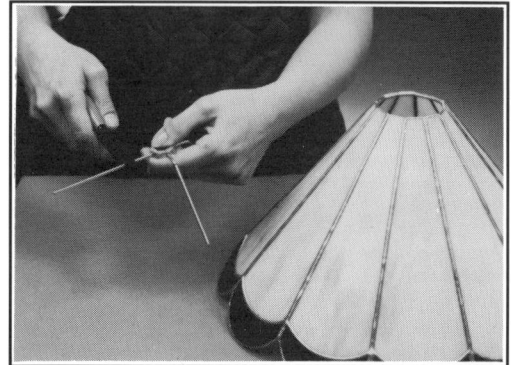

Installation:

Step 1: To ensure the spider hole is centered, measure the top opening of your lampshade and divide this dimension by two. For example, a 4" opening divided by two is 2". Measure this distance from the center of the spider's central-hole down an arm and mark with a pen. Measure and mark all arms.

Step 2: Use a pair of pliers to bend the arms down at the marks. The angle of the bend must match the top angle of the lampshade. The first trial bend is simply a guess at the correct angle.

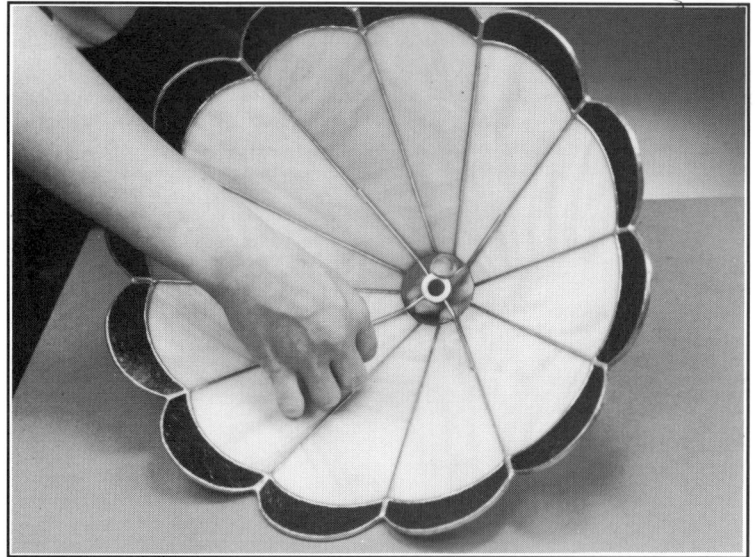

Step 3: Gently turn the lamp upside down and test the arm angles by positioning and centering the spider in the shade opening. Adjust the angles as needed. Each arm should extend approximately two to four inches from the top of the opening and straight down each seam, cut them shorter if necessary.

Step 4: When the spider fits the opening correctly, remove and tin each arm from the bend to the outside tip. Position and center the spider into the shade opening and solder the arms securely down the inside seams.

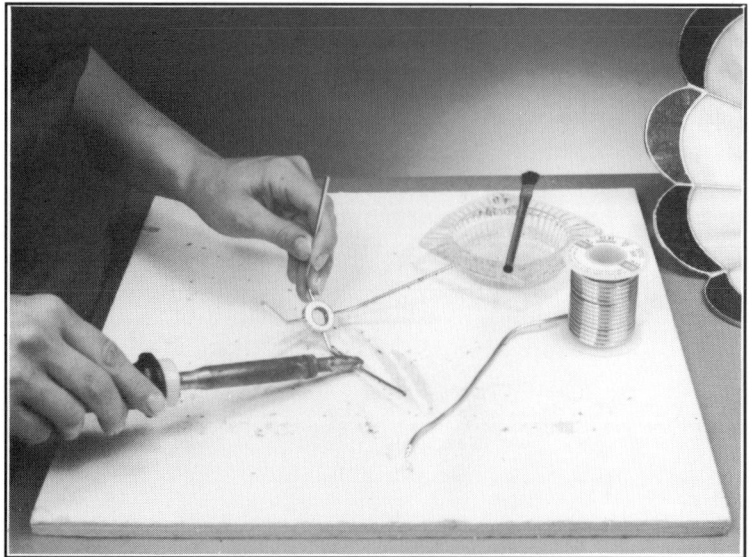

12

VASE CAPS

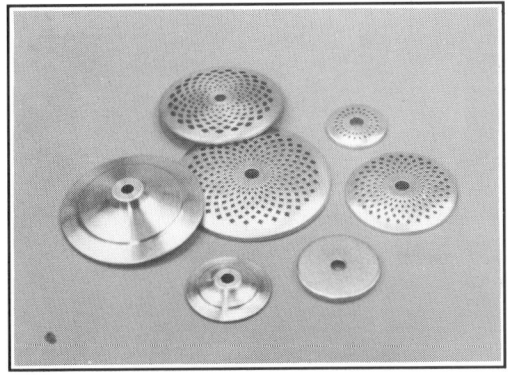

These are brass (or copper) disks which are available in various sizes. They can be plain or ventilated with fancy designs. The size must be matched to the shade top diameter.

INSTALLATION

Step 1: To install a cap properly it should fit just inside the shade opening. This will ensure that it is soldered securely to the vertical seams of the lampshade. Vase caps are manufactured in standard sizes and often the shade opening is an odd size. Most vase caps can be cut down with sheet metal shears to custom fit the opening.

Step 2: If you were unable to find a cap to fit the shade opening exactly, choose a cap which is slightly larger than the opening. To mark the cap for trimming, place it on the shade opening from the outside and use a felt-tip pen to trace around the opening from the inside.

Step 3: Trim the cap following the traced line with sheet metal shears (tin snips). Place the cap back on the shade to check the fit and adjust as necessary.

Step 4: The outside surface of the vase cap should be *tinned* with a thin layer of solder before installation. Tinning will allow antique patina (see Page 14) to color the cap the same as the rest of the solder seams. It will also make soldering the cap to the shade easier.

NOTE: Since the vase cap draws heat away from the soldering area (referred to as heatsinking) it is more difficult to make the solder flow. To ensure a smooth finish, more time will be required to heat both solder and metal while tinning.

Step 5: Position the cap on the shade opening and tack solder it. The cap must be centered and level on the shade. When the fit is correct, solder around the cap inside and out.

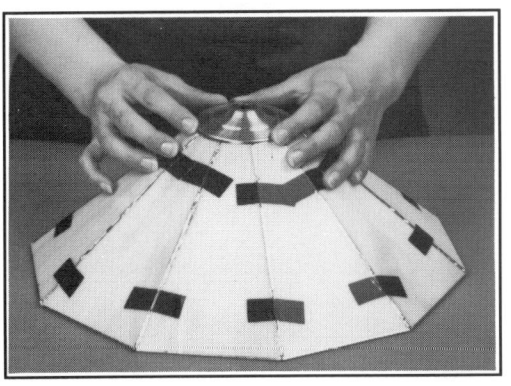

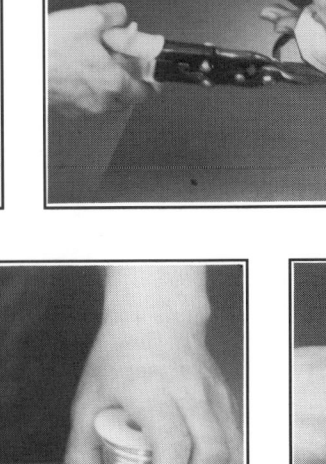

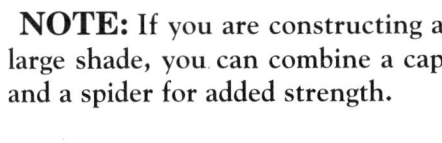

NOTE: If you are constructing a large shade, you can combine a cap and a spider for added strength.

WARNING: When wiring and installing your lamp you must consider all federal and local electrical codes and regulations.

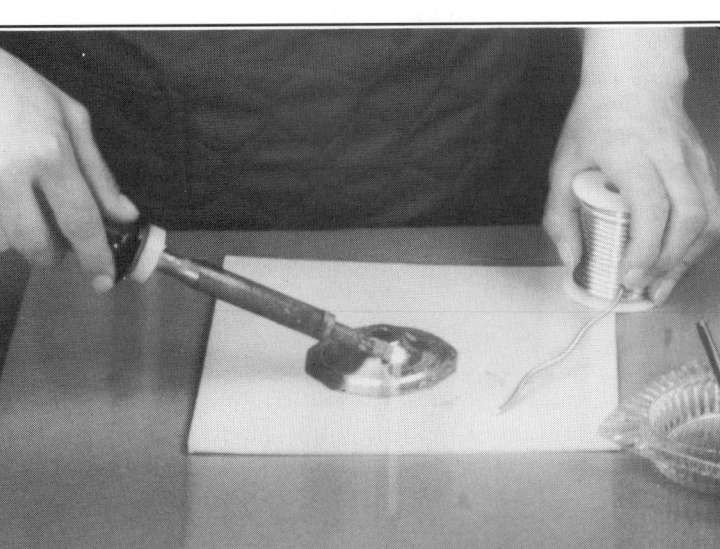

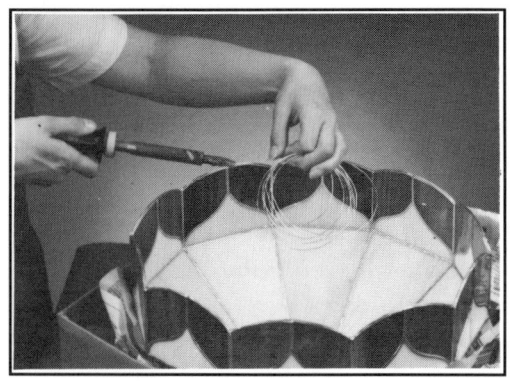

CLEANING YOUR PROJECT

It is very important to clean your project as soon as you have finished working on it. If the flux is left on, it will corrode the solder even overnight. This will make touch-up soldering or final clean-up difficult. Any good quality glass cleaner will work, as will a solution of vinegar and water.

If the solder has corroded and is difficult to solder they can be cleaned by scrubbing with fine steel wool or a small wire brush. Caution: If you have already applied antique patina to the solder, scrubbing will remove it.

WIRE SUPPORT AROUND BOTTOM OF LAMP

It is recommended that a wire (14-18 gauge, brass or copper) be soldered around the bottom edge of your lamp for reinforcement. This wire will help to finish the bottom edge and holds it firmly together. Tack solder one piece of wire completely around the bottom edge and overlap the ends at least 1/2 inch. Finish the edge with a solder bead.

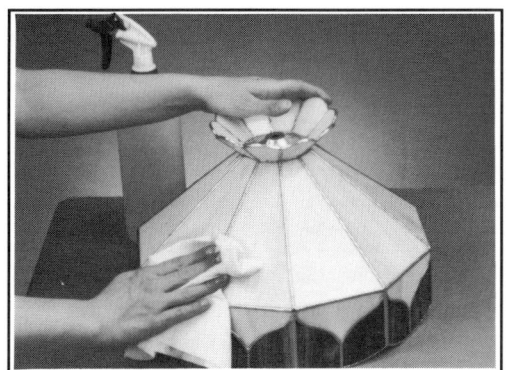

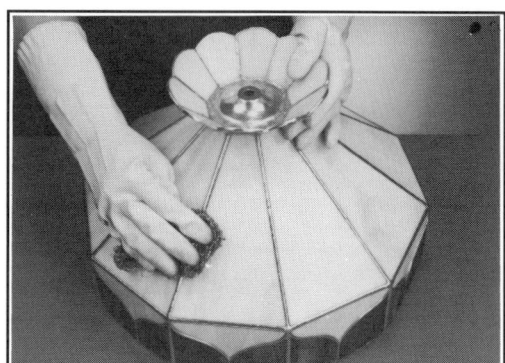

POLISHING OR WAXING

To preserve the shiny finish on the solder after a patina has been applied, use a good quality spray furniture polish. Apply the polish and rub all solder seams vigorously. For an even shinier finish, polish the patina with a jeweler's rouge cloth or use a brass or silver polish. Finish with an application of car wax. You can even polish the wax with a power car polisher.

ANTIQUE PATINA

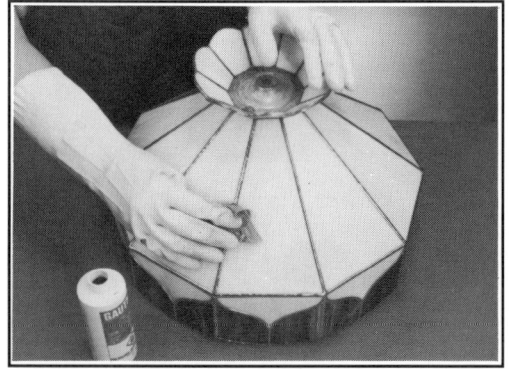

Best results are achieved when patina is applied to solder immediately after it is completed and cleaned with glass cleaner. Rub the solder using a soft rag or brush soaked with the liquid patina. Clean the solution from the glass immediately. Wear rubber gloves while handling this solution. If your project has been finished for a few days, you must scrub down all the soldered seams with fine steel wool or a metal pot scrubber and clean to remove all corrosion before applying the patina.

PHOTOCOPYING YOUR PATTERNS

In recent years the photocopier has come into very wide use for many applications. Local copy centers are opening everywhere, offering services that include enlarging and reducing your originals. This opens up a multitude of possibilities for the stained glass crafter to alter the size of patterns quickly and easily. Enlarging is especially useful for free-form projects such as sun catchers or small panels due to the limitation in size, depending on the photocopier used.

There is, however, one note of caution concerning the use of photocopiers (other than possible copyright infringement). Most photocopiers do not make exact copies of the original. While the copy is very close, the mechanics of the copying process introduces some amount of distortion that can be disastrous when constructing a three-dimensional project such as a lampshade. The distortion usually results in a slight enlargement (or reduction) of the pattern in the vertical dimension to a greater degree than in the horizontal dimension. This does not mean you cannot use a photocopier for your lamp patterns, but it does mean you must carefully measure each pattern component to verify that they will fit one to the other.

RIBBONS II by Charles Knapp

PROJECT 1

DEGREE OF DIFFICULTY
1 | **2** | 3 | 4 | 5

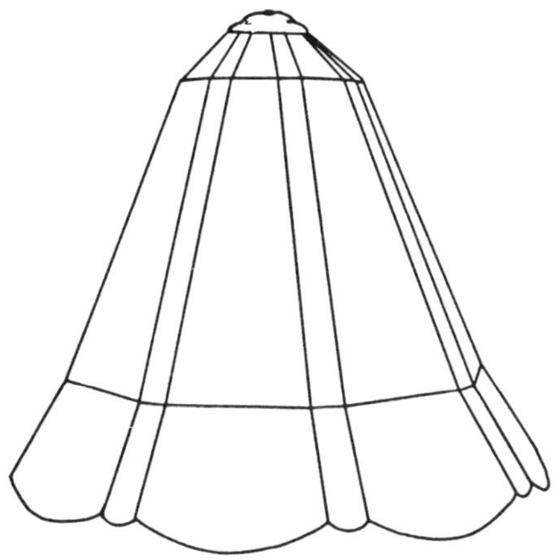

SPECIFICATIONS
# pieces—	48
# sides—	16
Height—	9" (23 cm)
Bottom Diameter—	10" (25 cm)
Top Diameter—	1 1/2" (4 cm)

LAMPBASE INFORMATION:
Base height — 8"
Harp size — 7 1/2"

MATERIALS
- — 2 sq. ft. Streaky Gray Opal
- — 3/4 sq. ft. Dark Red Cathedral

PATTERN ON PAGE 16

PROJECT INFORMATION: Due to the top angle of the lampshade, a 1/2" or 1" harp extender or riser is required to make allowance for lampbase harp.

ELEGANCE by Linda Holmes

PROJECT 2

DEGREE OF DIFFICULTY
1 | 2 | **3** | 4 | 5

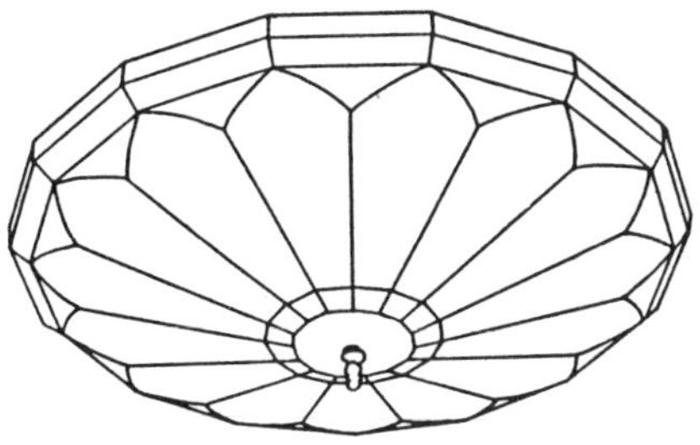

SPECIFICATIONS
# pieces—	75
# sides—	15
Depth—	3 3/4" (9.5 cm)
Bottom Diameter—	17 1/2" (44 cm)
Top Diameter—	3" (8 cm)

PATTERN ON PAGE 17

MATERIALS
- — 3 sq. ft. White Opal
- — 1 1/4 sq. ft. Iridescent White Opal

PROJECT INFORMATION: It is not advisable to eliminate the small square at the top of the main body as it gives the lamp extra strength. Solder a reinforcement wire around the outside edge of the lamp. For Inverted Lamp Installation see page 11.

Project 1 · RIBBONS II

Cut 8 of Each

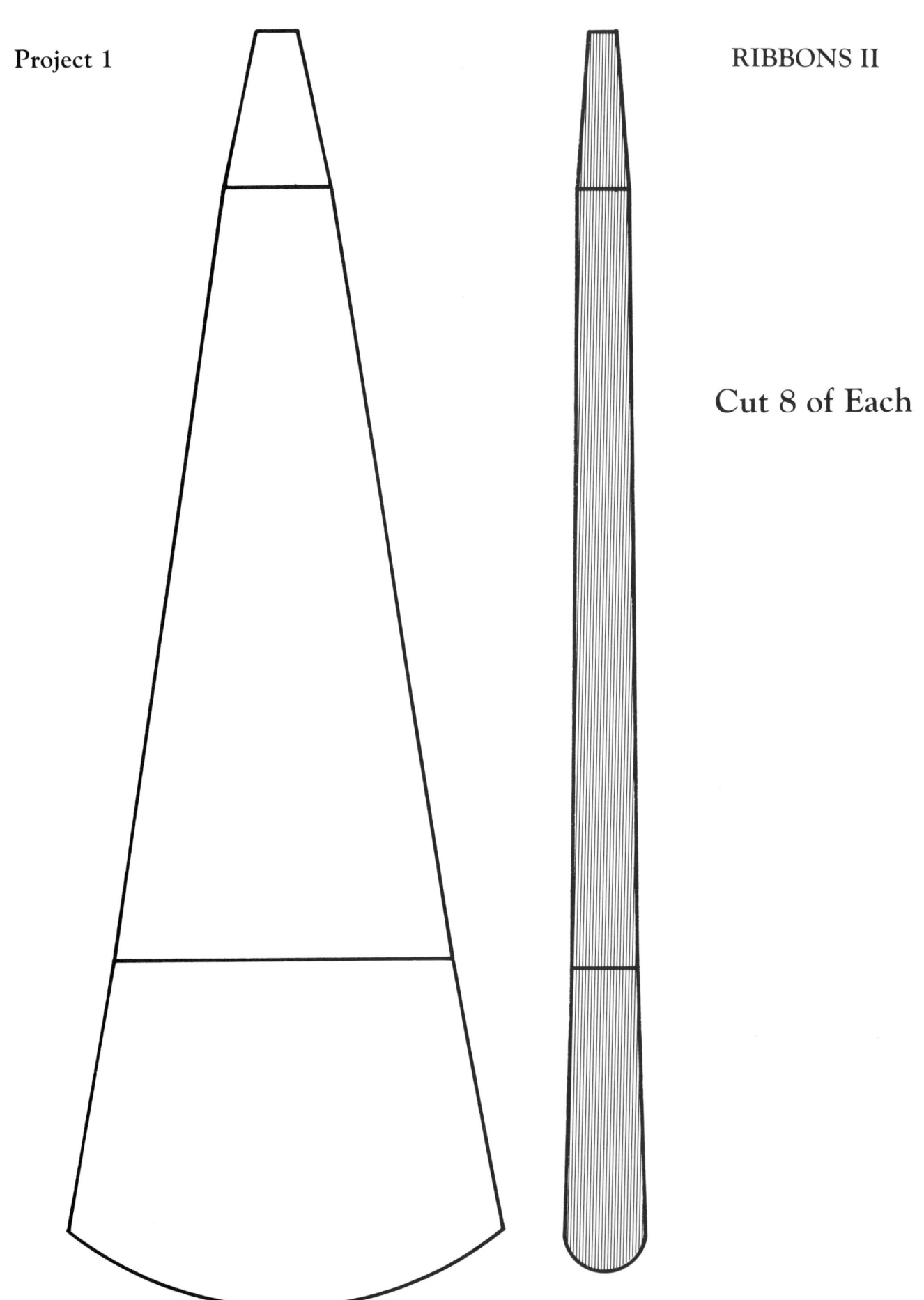

Project 2 ELEGANCE

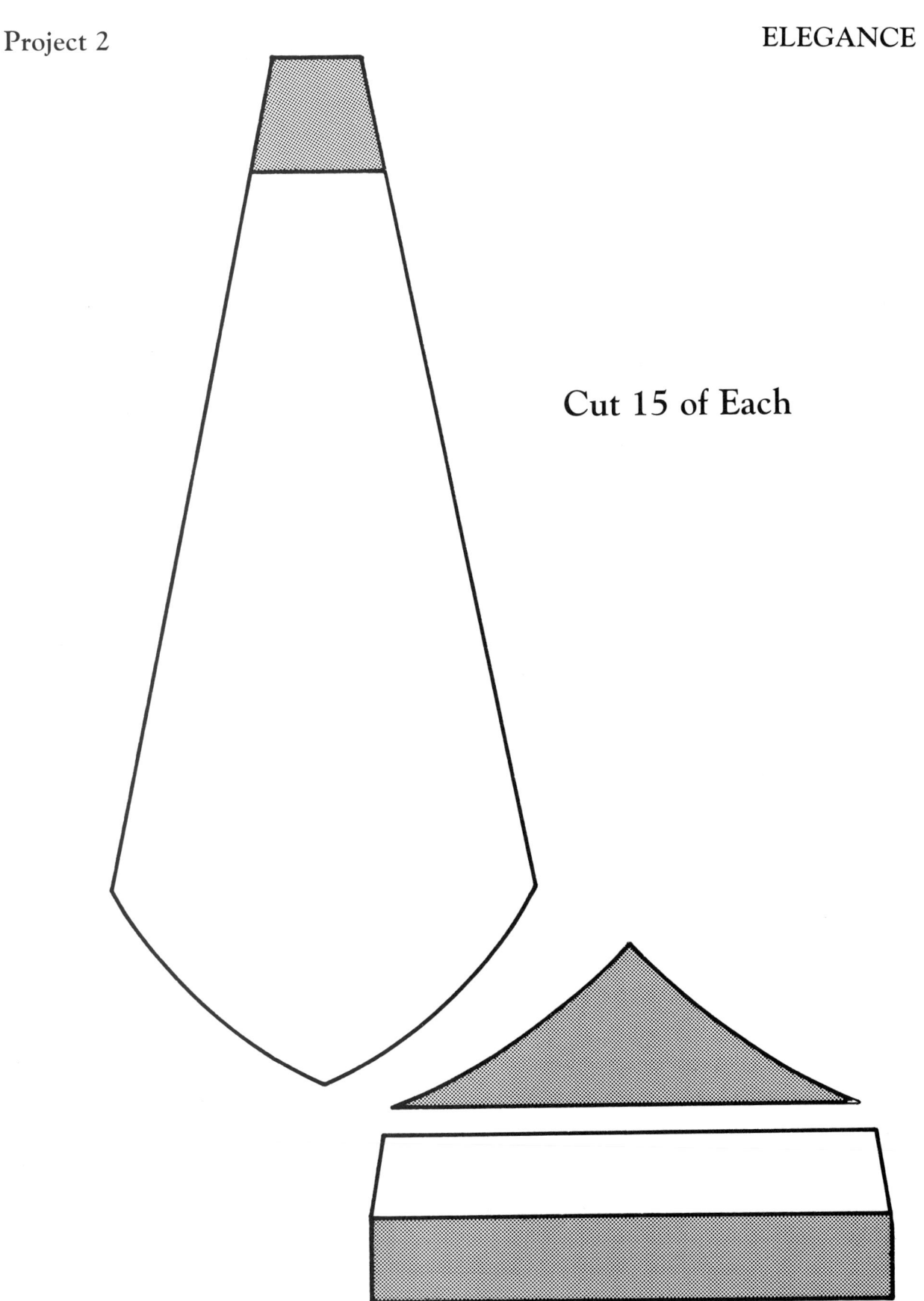

Cut 15 of Each

COUNTRY DOME   by Linda Holmes

PROJECT 3

DEGREE OF DIFFICULTY: 1 | 2 | 3 | **4** | 5

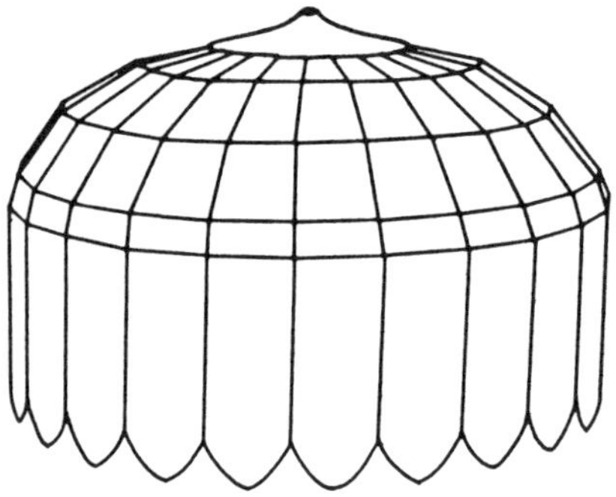

SPECIFICATIONS

# pieces—	120
# sides—	24
Height—	8" (20 cm)
Bottom Diameter—	12" (30 cm)
Top Diameter—	4" (10 cm)

PATTERN ON PAGE 19

MATERIALS

- ▨ — 3 sq. ft. White Opal
- ☐ — 1/3 sq. ft Textured Light Blue Opal

PROJECT INFORMATION: This lampshade is suitable for both swag or base.

PRESTIGE   by Randy & Judy Wardell

PROJECT 4

DEGREE OF DIFFICULTY: 1 | 2 | **3** | 4 | 5

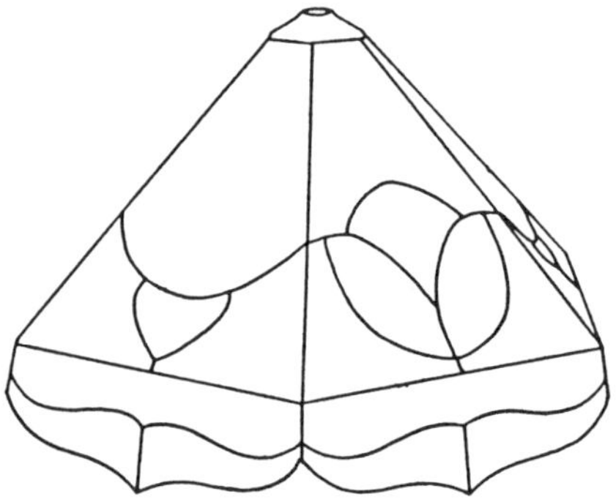

SPECIFICATIONS

# pieces—	48
# sides—	6
Height—	9" (23 cm)
Bottom Diameter—	13 1/2" (34 cm)
Top Diameter—	2" (5 cm)

PATTERN ON PAGES 20 & 21

MATERIALS

- ☐ — 3 sq. ft. Clear Glue Chip
- ▨ — 1 sq. ft. Textured Clear

Bevels —
4 — 4" x 4" Clusters

Bevel Alternative—
3/4 sq. ft. Cathedral

PROJECT INFORMATION:
This lamp requires a stylized tupil bevel cluster as the pattern indicates. The triangle bevel in the alternating panel comes as part of the tulip cluster. You can substitute any bevel cluster that does not exceed 4" x 4" in size.

Project 3   COUNTRY DOME

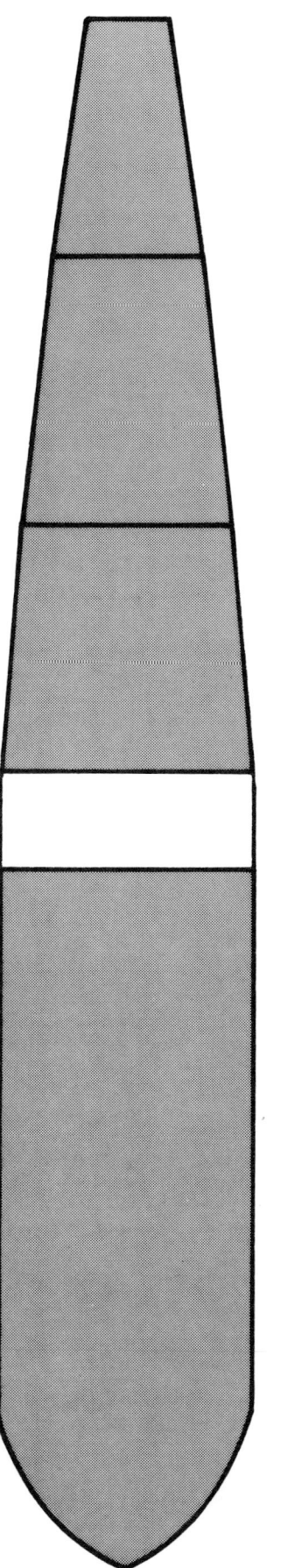

Cut 24 of Each

19

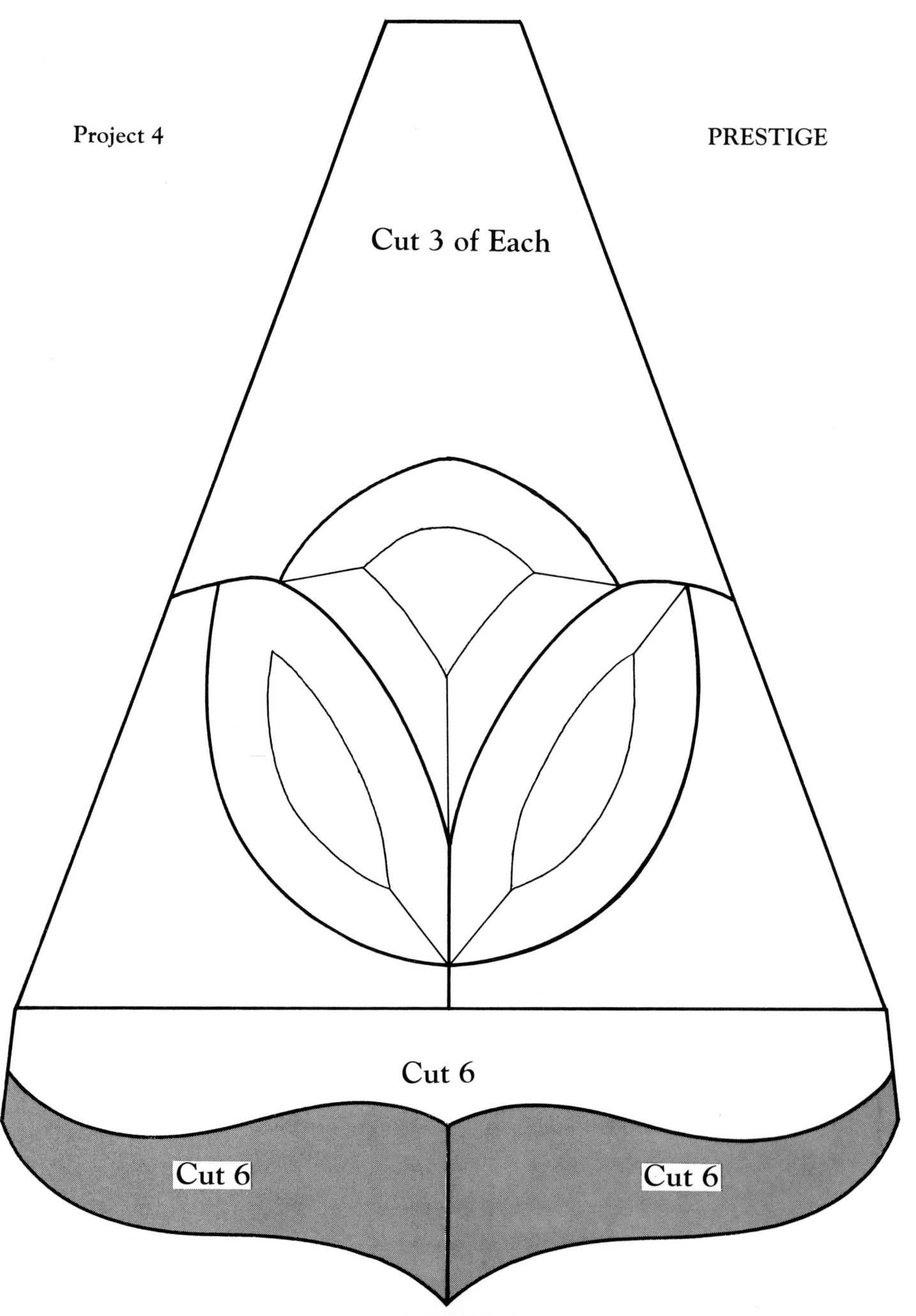

Project 4   PRESTIGE

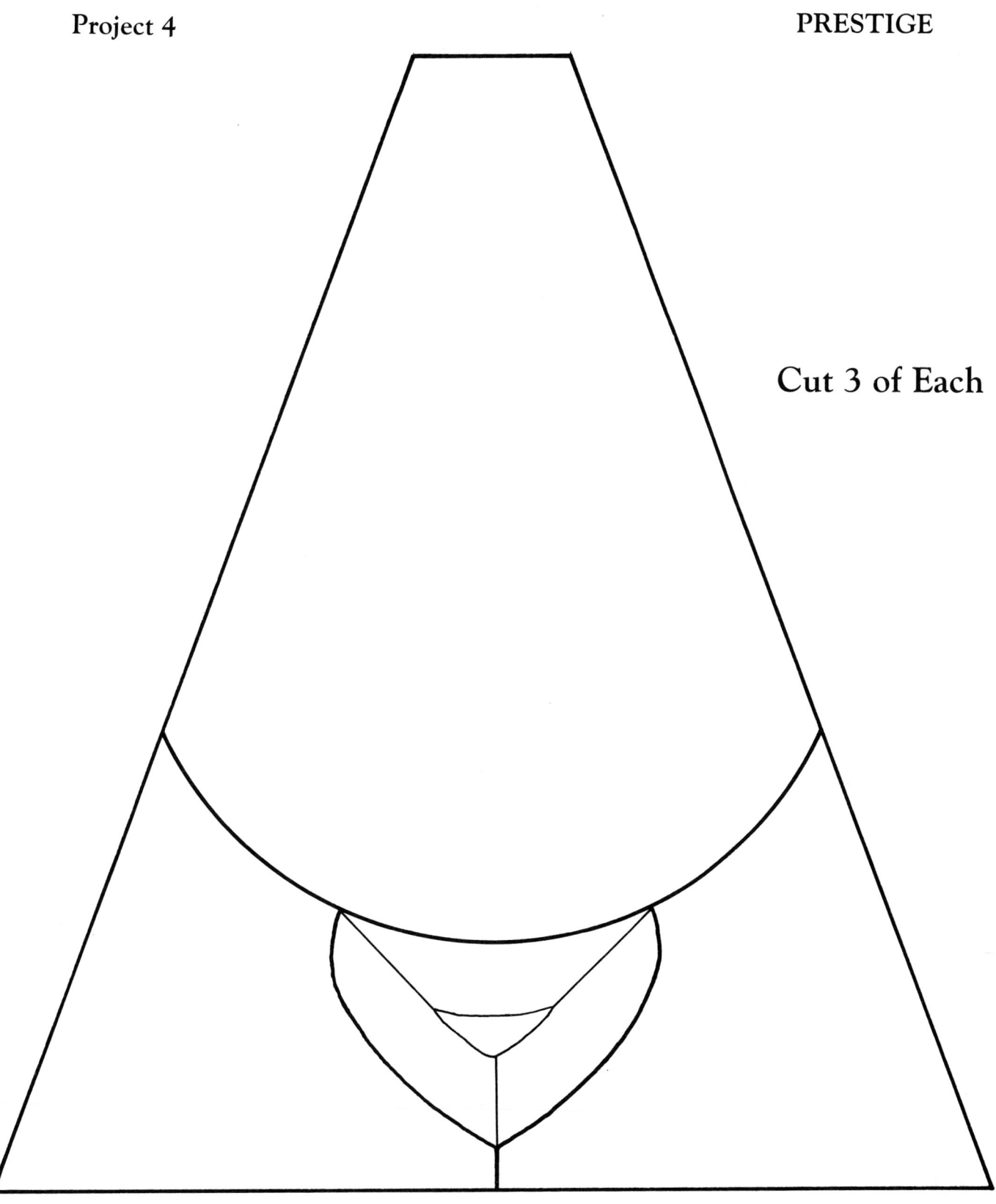

Cut 3 of Each

SWEET DREAMS   by Linda Holmes

PROJECT 5

DEGREE OF DIFFICULTY
1 | 2 | 3 | 4 | 5

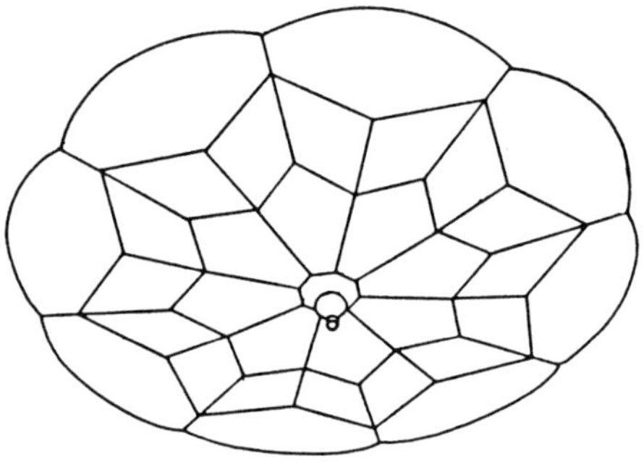

SPECIFICATIONS

- # pieces— 32
- # sides— 8
- Depth— 1 1/2" (4 cm)
- Bottom Diameter— 15 1/2" (39 cm)
- Top Diameter— 1 1/2" (4 cm)

PATTERN ON PAGE 23

MATERIALS

- — 2 1/4 sq. ft. Wispy White Opal
- — 1 1/4 sq. ft. White/Pink/Green Fractures & Streamers

PROJECT INFORMATION: It is recommended that a reinforcement wire be soldered along the seams between the main body and outside row to give the lamp extra strength. A brass ball chain (the type used on electrical pull-chain sockets) has been soldered to the outside edge of this lamp instead of a wire. If using the ball chain you will require 4 1/2 feet. For Inverted Lamp Installation see page 11.

MALLARD DUCK   by Linda Holmes

PROJECT 6

DEGREE OF DIFFICULTY
1 | 2 | 3 | **4** | 5

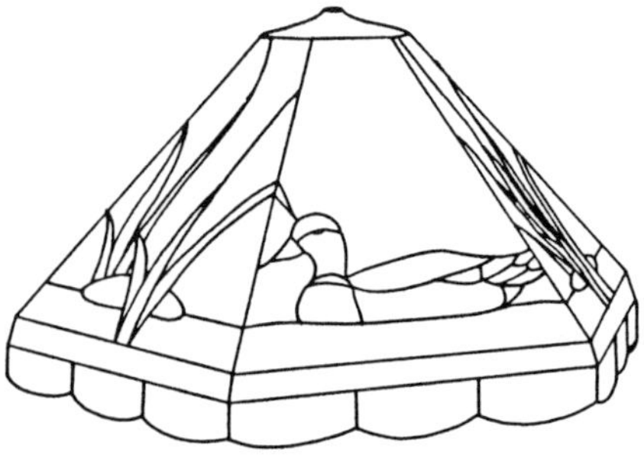

SPECIFICATIONS

- # pieces— 135
- # sides— 6
- Height— 8 1/2" (22 cm)
- Bottom Diameter— 14" (36 cm)
- Top Diameter— 3 1/2" (9 cm)

PATTERN ON PAGES 24 & 25

MATERIALS

- — 3 1/2 sq. ft Mottled Medium Blue Opal
- — 1/2 sq. ft. Textured Dark Blue Cathedral
- — 3/4 sq. ft. Green/Brown Opal
- — 1/4 sq. ft White Opal
- Sm. Pc.—Brown/Gray Opal
- Sm. Pc.—Iridescent Cath. Green
- Sm. Pc.—Rust Opal
- Sm. Pc.—Black Cathedral
- Sm. Pc.—Blue Opal
- Sm. Pc.—Gray Opal
- Sm. Pc.—Yellow/Green Opal

PROJECT INFORMATION: The eye detail shown in the photograph is an overlay of copper foil. There are many other items available you can use to create this feature such as a small solder glob, cut glass, commercial glass eyes, paint, etc.. To fasten these items to your project (except the paint) use clear silicone seal, white bond glue or epoxy.

Project 5　　　　　　　　　　　　　　　　　　　　　　　　SWEET DREAMS

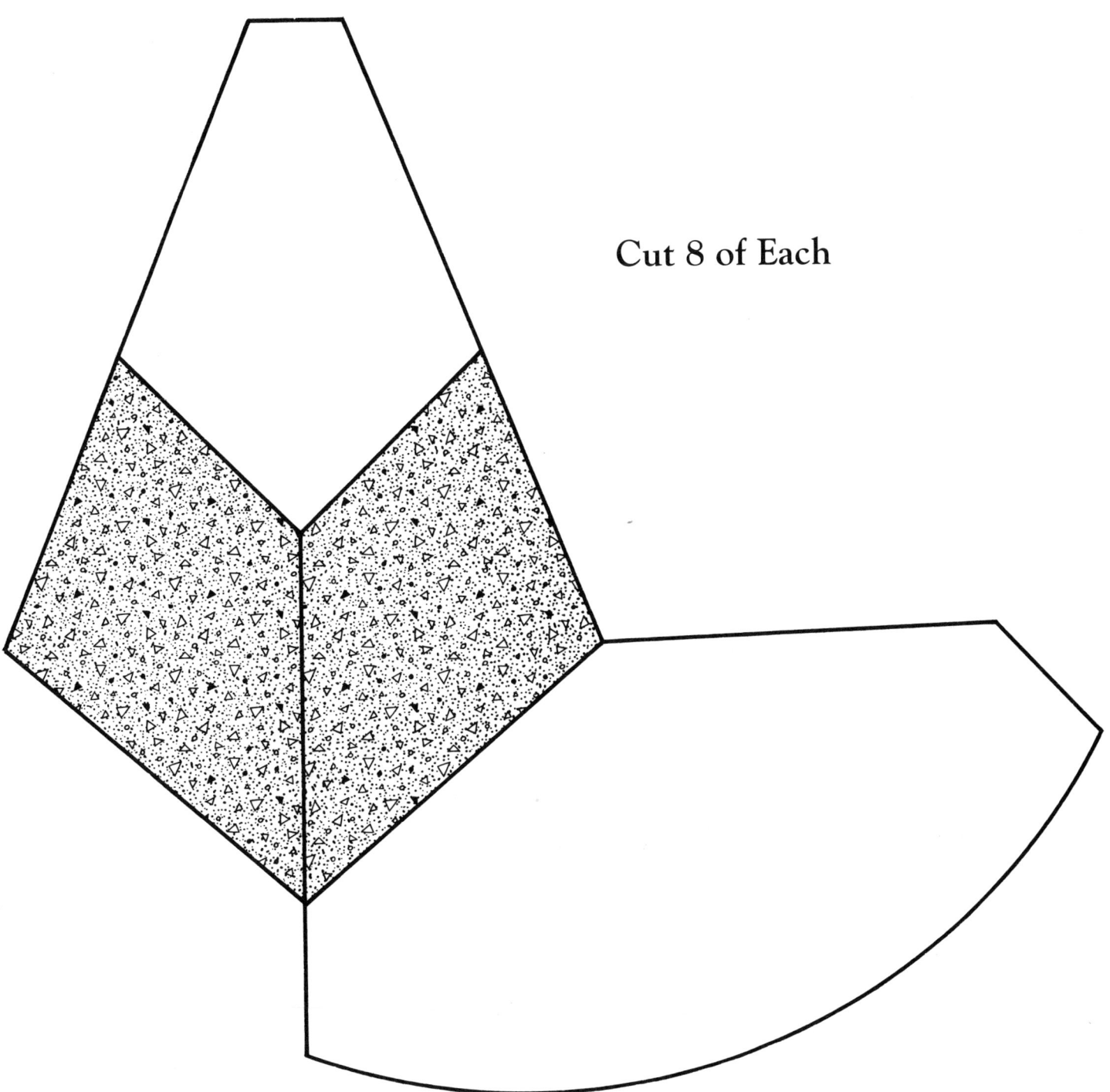

Cut 8 of Each

23

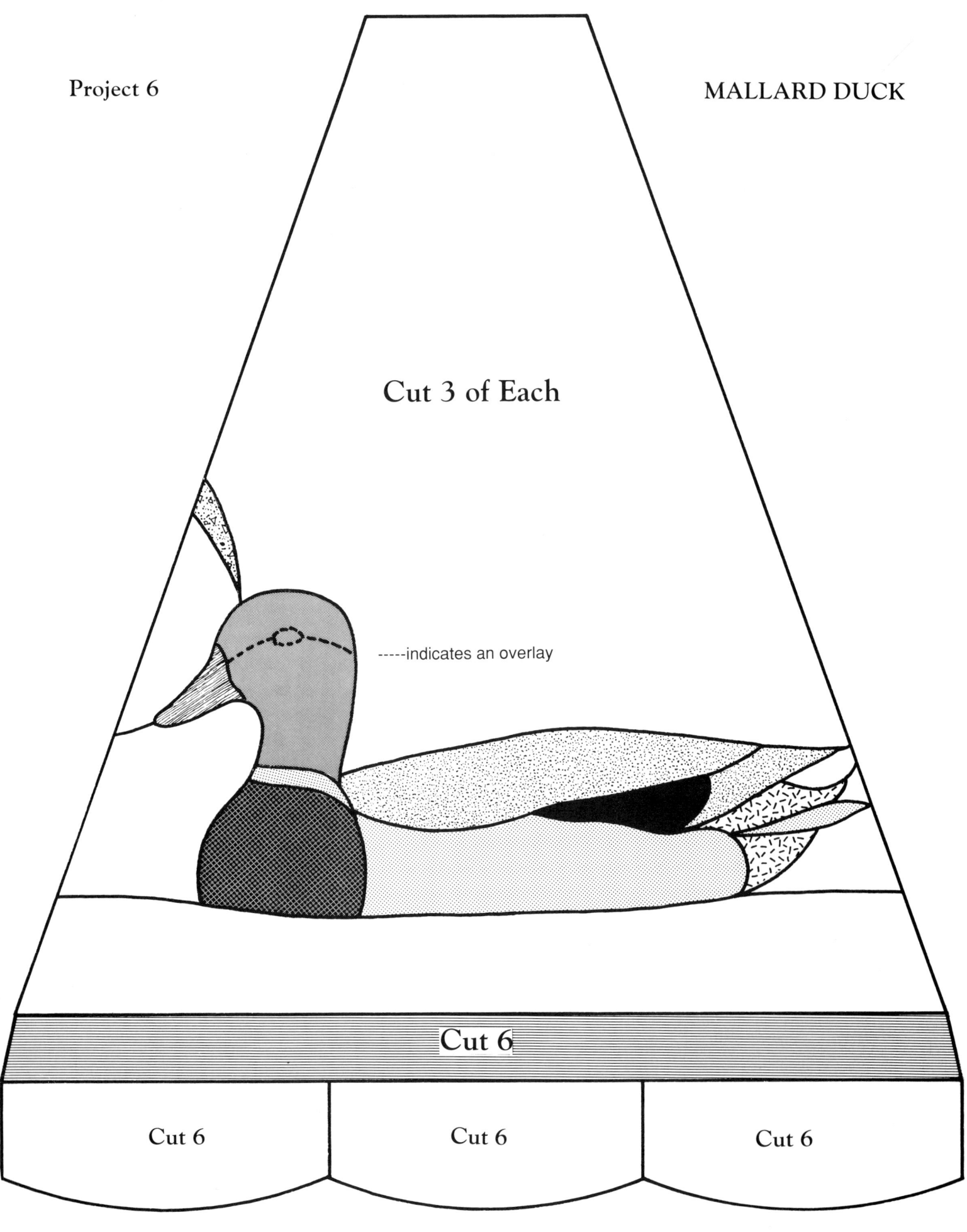

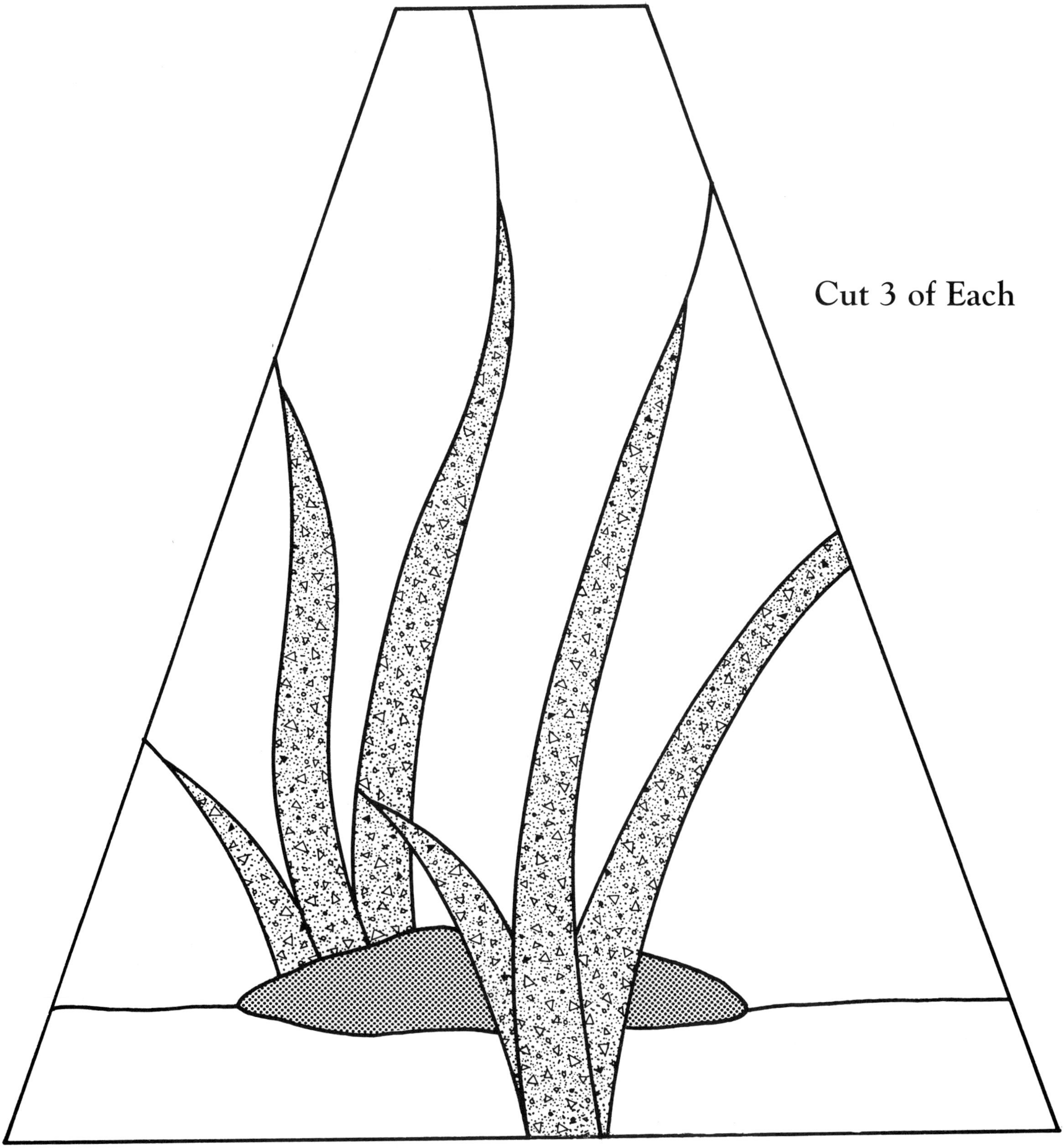

Project 6 MALLARD DUCK

Cut 3 of Each

25

| **THERESA'S FLOWER** | by Charles Knapp | PROJECT 7 |

DEGREE OF DIFFICULTY: 1 | 2 | **3** | 4 | 5

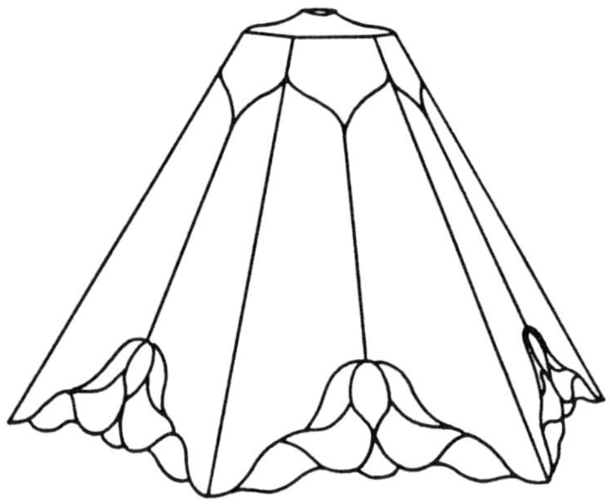

SPECIFICATIONS
- # pieces— 66
- # sides— 6
- Height— 9 1/2" (24 cm)
- Bottom Diameter— 11" (28 cm)
- Top Diameter— 3" (8 cm)

LAMPBASE INFORMATION:
- Base height — 6"
- Harp size — 7 1/2"

MATERIALS
- — 1/3 sq. ft. Iridescent Blue Opal
- — 1/3 sq. ft. Iridescent Streaky Pink Cathedral
- — 3/4 sq. ft. Streaky Pink/Amber Cathedral
- — 2 1/2 sq. ft. Streaky Pink/Blue/Amber Opal

PATTERN ON PAGE 27

PROJECT INFORMATION: The top opening should be fitted with a 3 1/2" round vase cap cut to fit as shown on page 13.

| **BEVEL BELTED CONE** | by Brian Eagle | PROJECT 8 |

DEGREE OF DIFFICULTY: **1** | 2 | 3 | 4 | 5

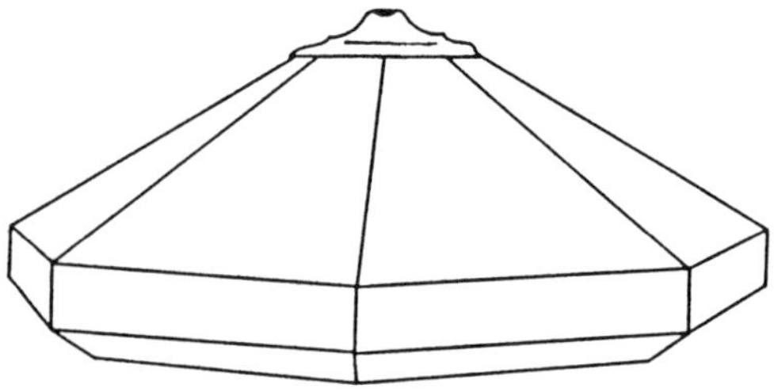

SPECIFICATIONS
- # pieces— 24
- # sides— 8
- Height— 8" (20 cm)
- Bottom Diameter— 21" (53 cm)
- Top Diameter— 5" (13 cm)

PATTERN ON PAGES 28 & 29

MATERIALS
- — 5 sq. ft. Streaky Black/Gray Opal

Bevels—8— 1 1/2" x 8"

Bevel Alternative—
1 sq. ft. Textured Clear or Gray Cathedral

PROJECT INFORMATION: The use of bevels in the trim band is optional. A contrasting glass as suggested in the material list can be substituted.

Project 7 THERESA'S FLOWER

Cut 6 of Each

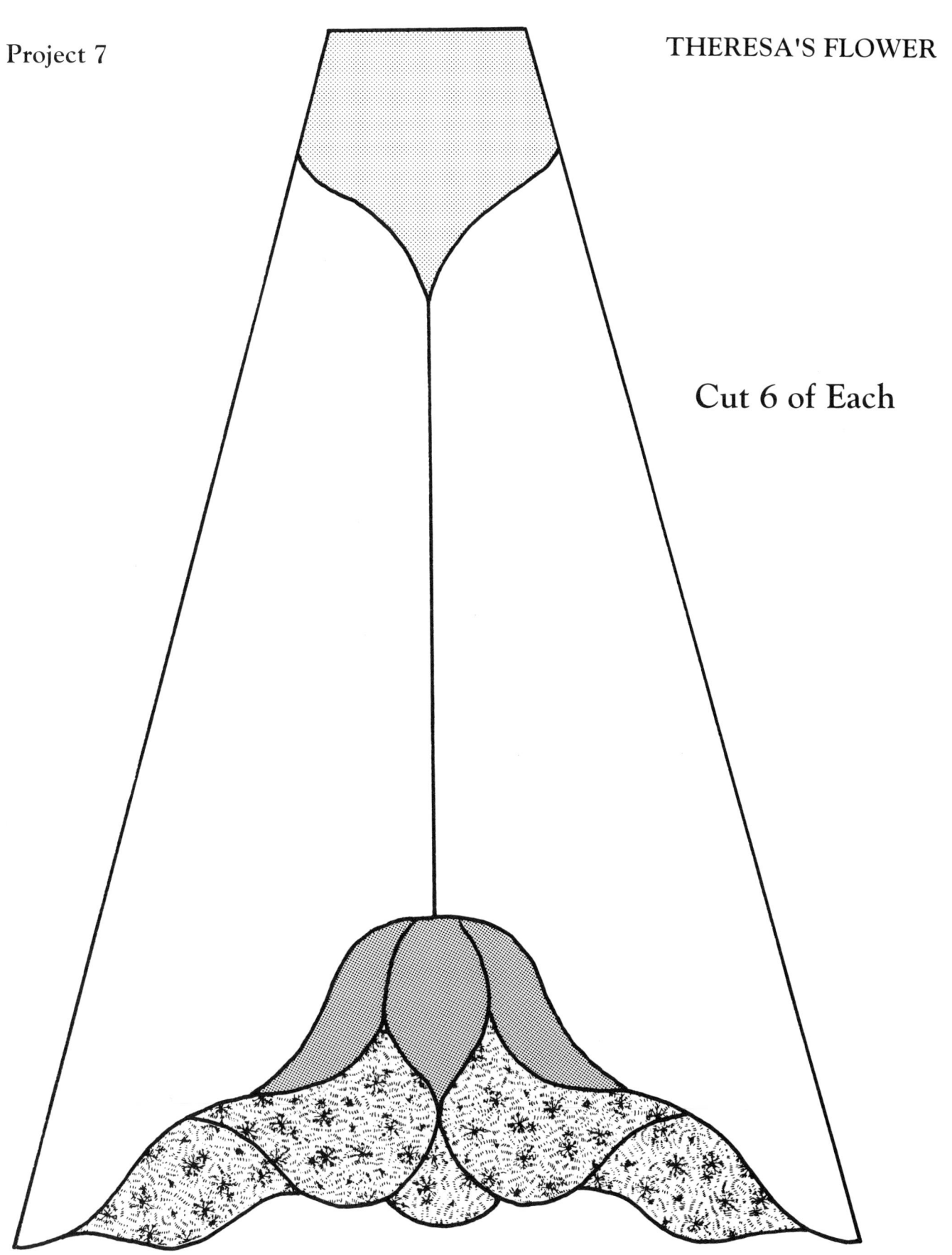

27

Project 8 BEVEL BELTED CONE

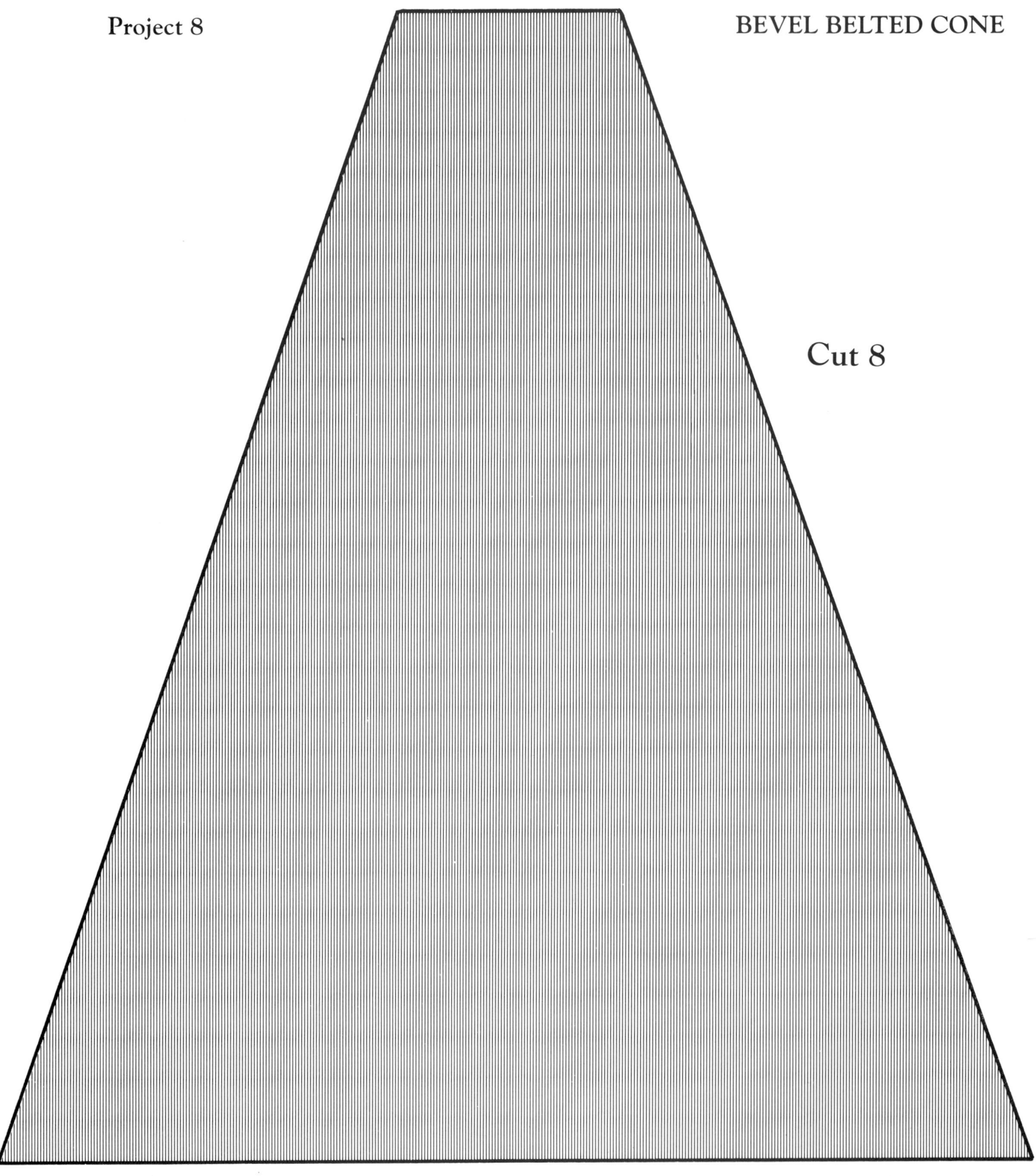

Cut 8

Project 8   BEVEL BELTED CONE

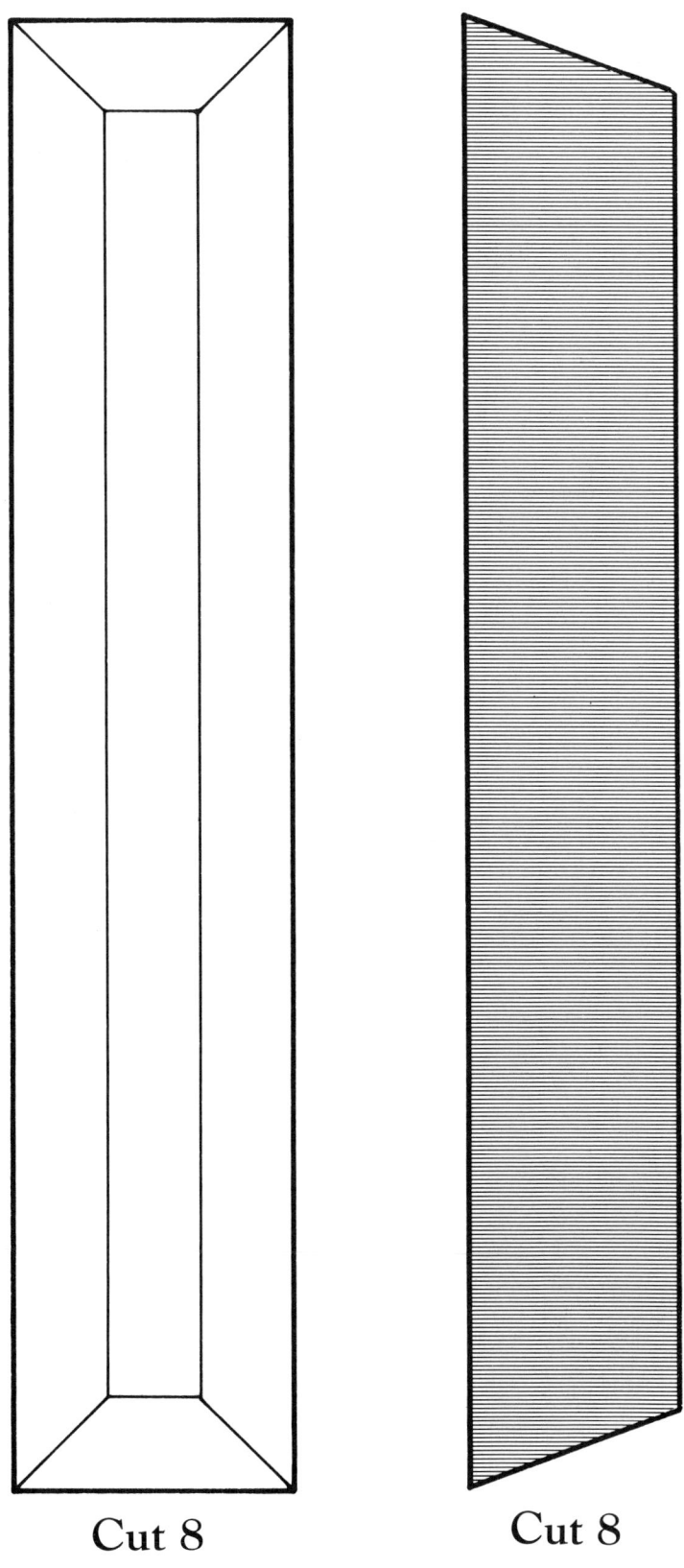

Cut 8   Cut 8

29

| **NOUVEAU CLASSIC** | by Brian Eagle | PROJECT 9 |

DEGREE OF DIFFICULTY
| 1 | **2** | 3 | 4 | 5 |

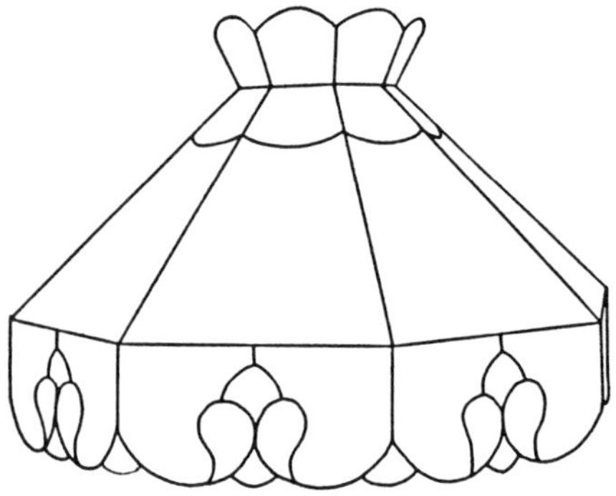

SPECIFICATIONS

# pieces—	80
# sides—	8
Height—	11"
	(28 cm)
Bottom Diameter—	15"
	(38 cm)
Top Diameter—	4"
	(10 cm)

PATTERN ON PAGES 30 & 31

MATERIALS

- □ — 4 1/2 sq. ft. Streaky Mauve/White Opal
- ▨ — 1/2 sq. ft. Light Mauve Cathedral
- ▦ — 1 sq. ft. Dark Mauve Cathedral

PROJECT INFORMATION: This lamp is suitable for either swag or base.

NOUVEAU CLASSIC

Cut 8 of Each

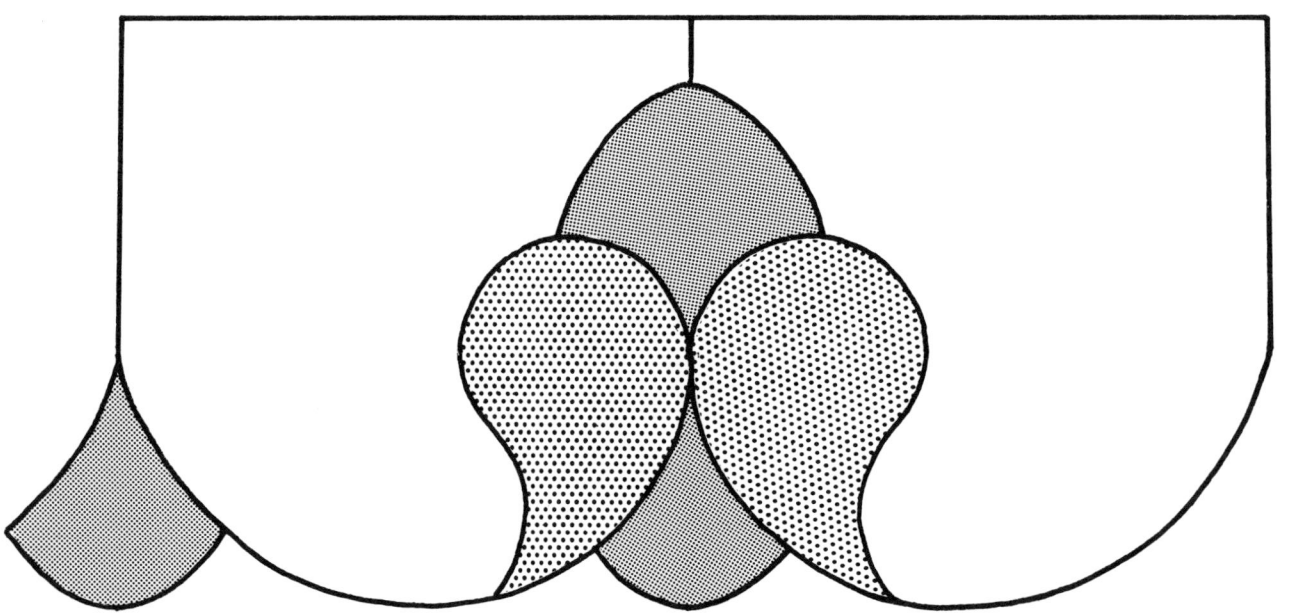

30

Project 9 NOUVEAU CLASSIC

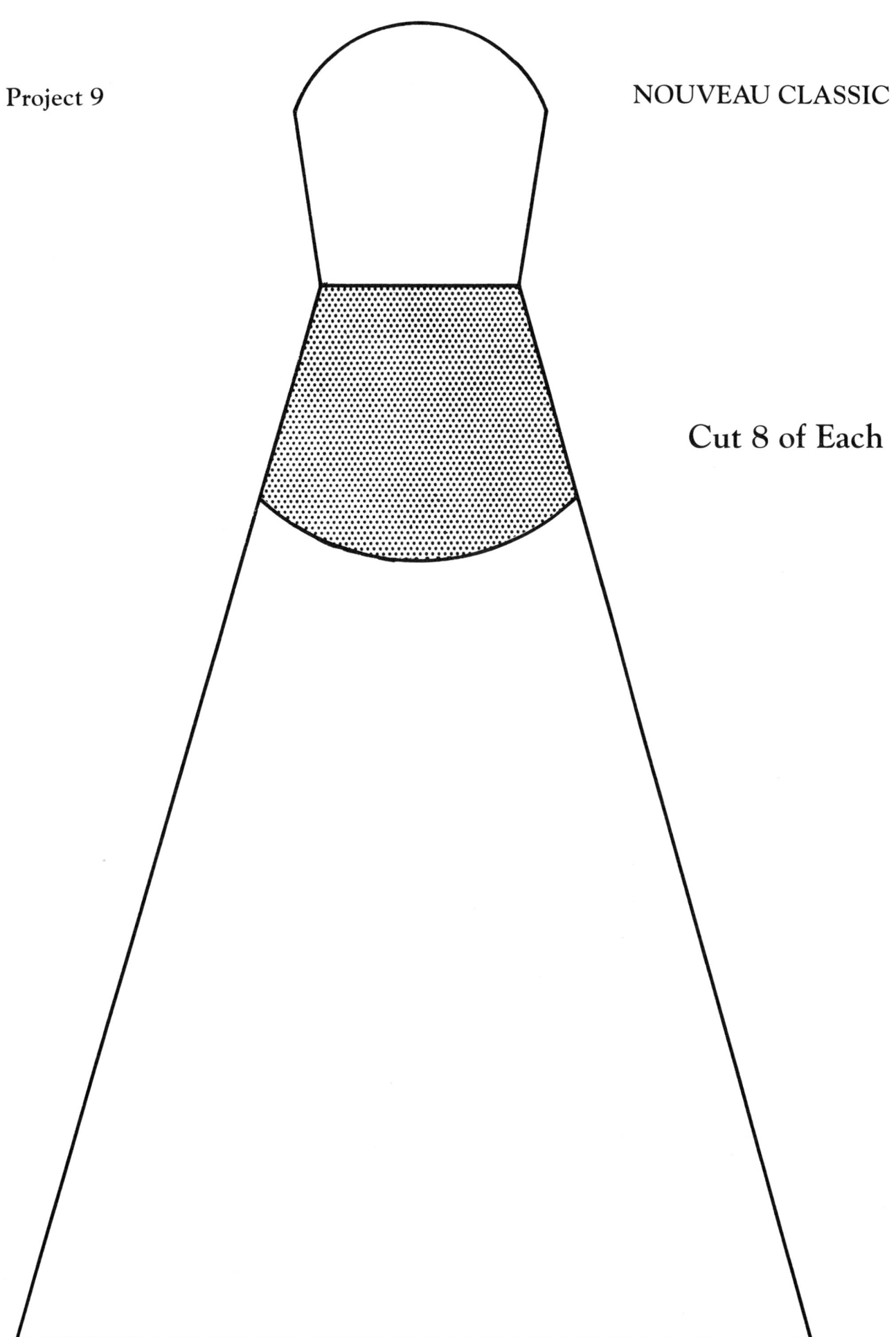

Cut 8 of Each

BARCELONA CONE   by Randy & Judy Wardell

PROJECT 10

DEGREE OF DIFFICULTY: 3 (of 1-5)

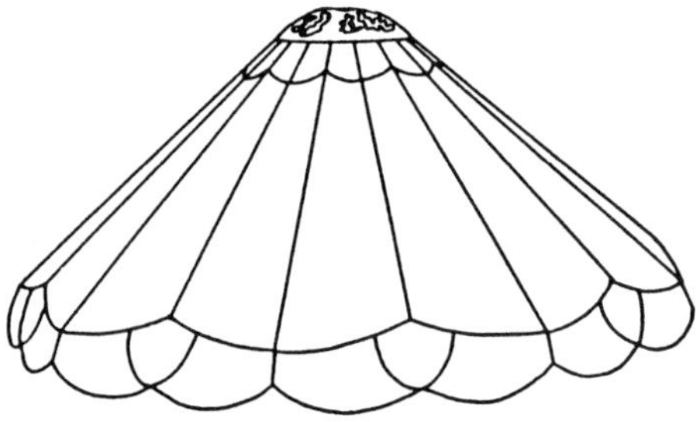

SPECIFICATIONS
- # pieces— 63
- # sides— 18
- Height— 9 1/2" (24 cm)
- Bottom Diameter— 21" (53 cm)
- Top Diameter— 4" (10 cm)

PATTERN ON PAGES 38 & 40

MATERIALS
- 4 1/2 sq. ft. Streaky Blue/Beige Opal
- 1/3 sq. ft. Cathedral Blue
- 1/3 sq. ft. Cathedral Mauve

PROJECT INFORMATION: In most cases, the joiner pattern piece will not fit accurately into its space. This is due to inevitable slight variations in glass cutting and assembly angle. Do not despair, go ahead and cut your glass according to the pattern supplied (it should be slightly larger than the space) and grind it to a perfect fit. For more information on Joiner Pieces see page 11.

OVERHEAD BLOOM   by Charles Knapp

PROJECT 11

DEGREE OF DIFFICULTY: 2 (of 1-5)

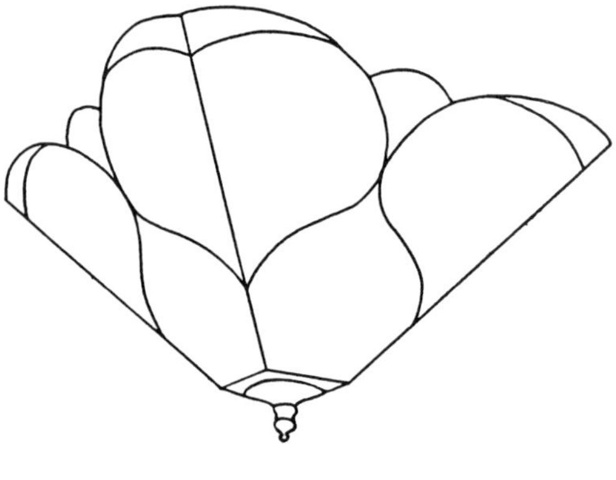

SPECIFICATIONS
- # pieces— 24
- # sides— 4
- Height— 9" (23 cm)
- Bottom Diameter— 16 1/2" (42 cm)
- Top Diameter-square 3 1/4" (8 cm)

PATTERN ON PAGE 39

MATERIALS
- 2 1/2 sq. ft. Streaky Green Opal
- 3 1/2 sq. ft. Streaky Beige Opal
- 3/4 sq. ft. Streaky Amber Cathedral

PROJECT INFORMATION: The top opening can be fitted with a 4 1/2" vase cap cut to fit as shown on page 13. This lampshade is suitable for both inverted or swag. For Inverted Lamp Installaton see page 11.

DRAPERY   by Charles Knapp

PROJECT 12

DEGREE OF DIFFICULTY
| 1 | 2 | **3** | 4 | 5 |

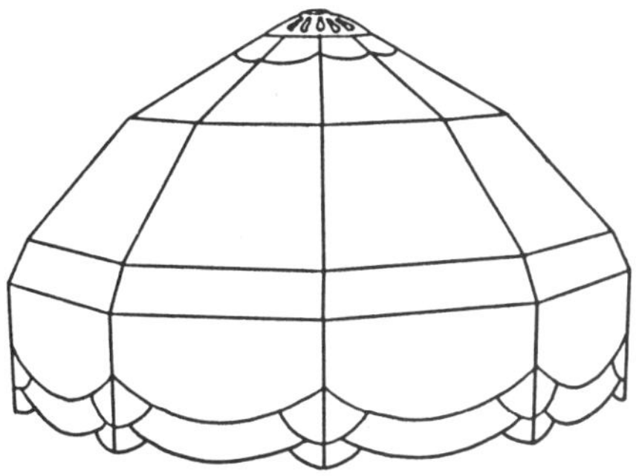

SPECIFICATIONS

- # pieces— 100
- # sides— 10
- Height— 11" (28 cm)
- Bottom Diameter— 18" (46 cm)
- Top Diameter— 3" (8 cm)

PATTERN ON PAGES 41 & 43

MATERIALS

- — 4 1/2 sq. ft. Red/Brown/Amber Streaky Opal
- — 1 sq. ft. Streaky Red/Amber Cathedral
- — 1 1/2 sq. ft. Dark Brown Textured Cathedral
- — 1/2 sq. ft. Gold Cathedral

PROJECT INFORMATION:
Although this lamp is rated as a Level 3 Degree of Difficulty the skill level can be reduced simply by leaving the main body and skirt sections plain.

LILY   by Brian Eagle

PROJECT 13

DEGREE OF DIFFICULTY
| 1 | 2 | **3** | 4 | 5 |

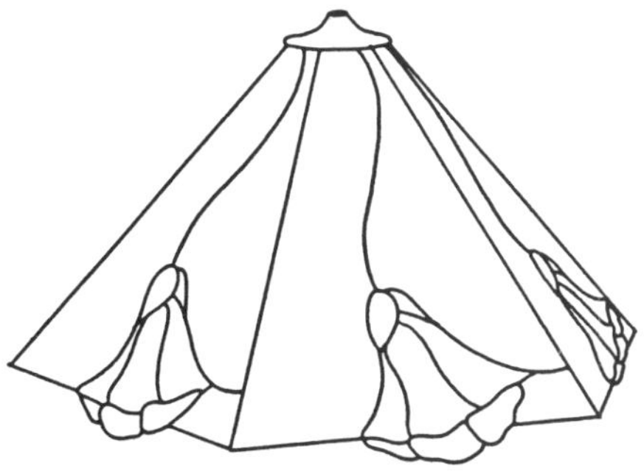

SPECIFICATIONS

- # pieces— 66
- # sides— 6
- Height— 12" (30 cm)
- Bottom Diameter— 19" (48 cm)
- Top Diameter— 3 1/2" (9 cm)

PATTERN ON PAGE 42

MATERIALS

- — 3 3/4 sq. ft. Clear/Green/Mauve Fractures & Streamers
- — 1 1/2 sq. ft. Textured Blue Cathedral
- — 1/4 sq. ft. Textured Green Cathedral

PROJECT INFORMATION: The top opening can be fitted with either a 3" six sided vase cap or a 3 1/2" round vase cap cut to fit as shown on page 13. The fractures & streamers glass shown in the photograph creates difficulty in cutting due to its texture. For a Level 2 Degree of Difficulty substitute a contrasting glass for the main body.

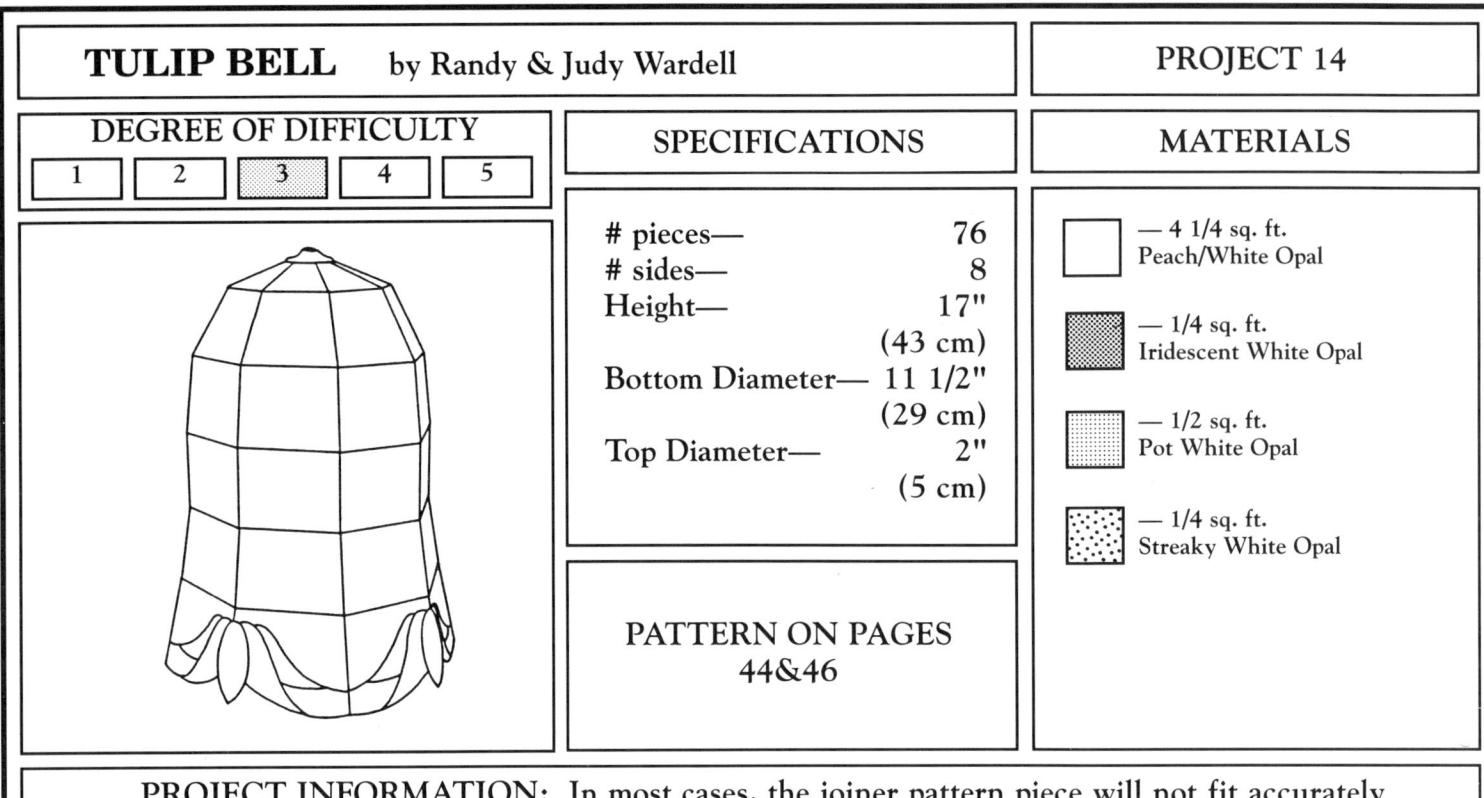

TULIP BELL   by Randy & Judy Wardell

PROJECT 14

DEGREE OF DIFFICULTY
1 | 2 | **3** | 4 | 5

SPECIFICATIONS
- # pieces— 76
- # sides— 8
- Height— 17" (43 cm)
- Bottom Diameter— 11 1/2" (29 cm)
- Top Diameter— 2" (5 cm)

PATTERN ON PAGES 44 & 46

MATERIALS
- — 4 1/4 sq. ft. Peach/White Opal
- — 1/4 sq. ft. Iridescent White Opal
- — 1/2 sq. ft. Pot White Opal
- — 1/4 sq. ft. Streaky White Opal

PROJECT INFORMATION: In most cases, the joiner pattern piece will not fit accurately into its space. This is due to inevitable slight variations in glass cutting and assembly angle. Do not despair, go ahead and cut your glass according to the pattern supplied (it should be slightly larger than the space) and grind it to a perfect fit. For more information on Joiner Pieces see page 11.

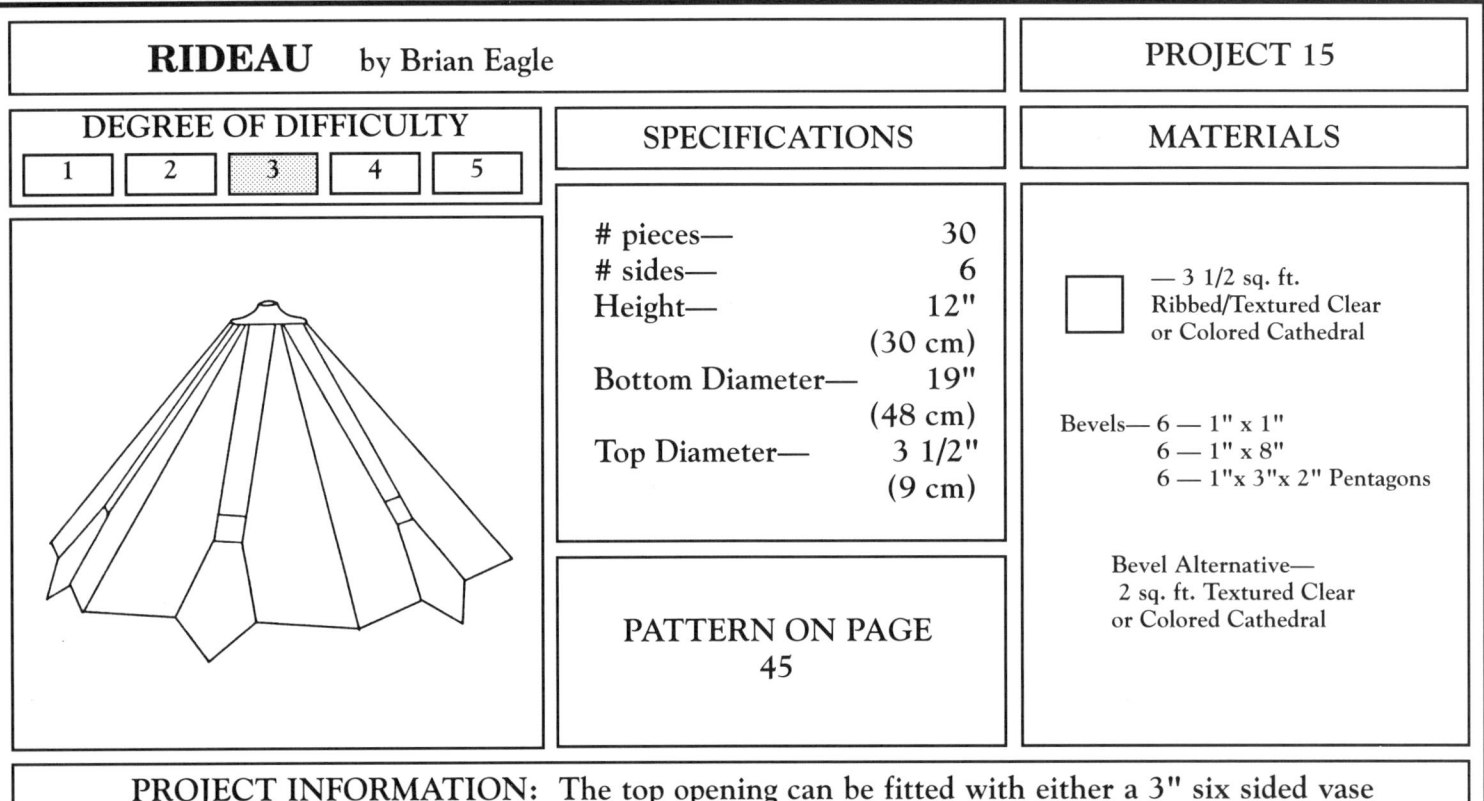

RIDEAU   by Brian Eagle

PROJECT 15

DEGREE OF DIFFICULTY
1 | 2 | **3** | 4 | 5

SPECIFICATIONS
- # pieces— 30
- # sides— 6
- Height— 12" (30 cm)
- Bottom Diameter— 19" (48 cm)
- Top Diameter— 3 1/2" (9 cm)

PATTERN ON PAGE 45

MATERIALS
- — 3 1/2 sq. ft. Ribbed/Textured Clear or Colored Cathedral

Bevels— 6 — 1" x 1"
6 — 1" x 8"
6 — 1" x 3" x 2" Pentagons

Bevel Alternative—
2 sq. ft. Textured Clear or Colored Cathedral

PROJECT INFORMATION: The top opening can be fitted with either a 3" six sided vase cap or a 3 1/2" round vase cap cut to fit as shown on page 13. The ribbed glass shown in the photograph is 4mm thick which creates some difficulty when cutting and grinding. For a Level 2 Degree of Difficulty substitute a textured clear of 3mm thickness or your favorite colored cathedral glass.

OLD ROSE by Randy & Judy Wardell		PROJECT 16
DEGREE OF DIFFICULTY 1 2 3 4 **5**	**SPECIFICATIONS**	**MATERIALS**

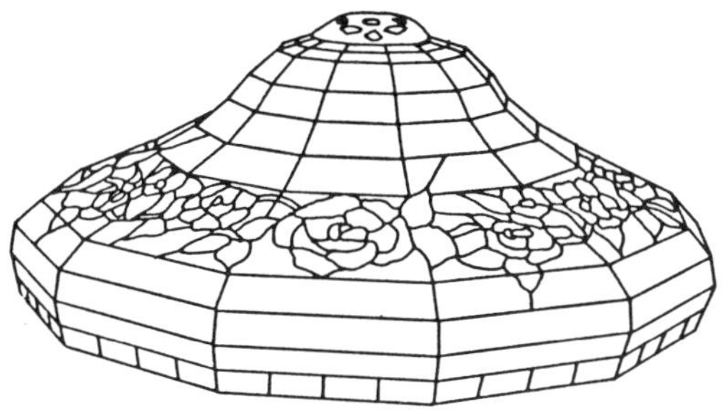

	SPECIFICATIONS	MATERIALS
(illustration of lamp)	# pieces— 468 # sides— 12 Height— 10" (25 cm) Bottom Diameter— 24" (61 cm) Top Diameter— 4" (10 cm) PATTERN ON PAGES 35, 36 & 37	— 4 sq. ft. Streaky Medium Beige Opal — 2 1/4 sq. ft. Streaky Light Beige Opal — 1/4 sq. ft. Beige/Brown Opal — 2 1/4 sq. ft. Pink/White Opal — 1 sq. ft. Pink Cathedral — 1 sq. ft. Streaky Green Opal — 1 sq. ft. Textured Green/Brown Opal — 1/4 sq. ft. Green Cathedral — Small Piece Yellow Opal

PROJECT INFORMATION: To begin assembly, start with the 2nd row from the top, then add the first row and solder the vase cap in place. In most cases, the joiner pattern piece will not fit accurately into its space. This is due to inevitable slight variations in glass cutting and assembly angle. Do not despair, go ahead and cut your glass according to the pattern supplied (it should be slightly larger than the space) and grind it to a perfect fit. For more information on Joiner Pieces see page 11.

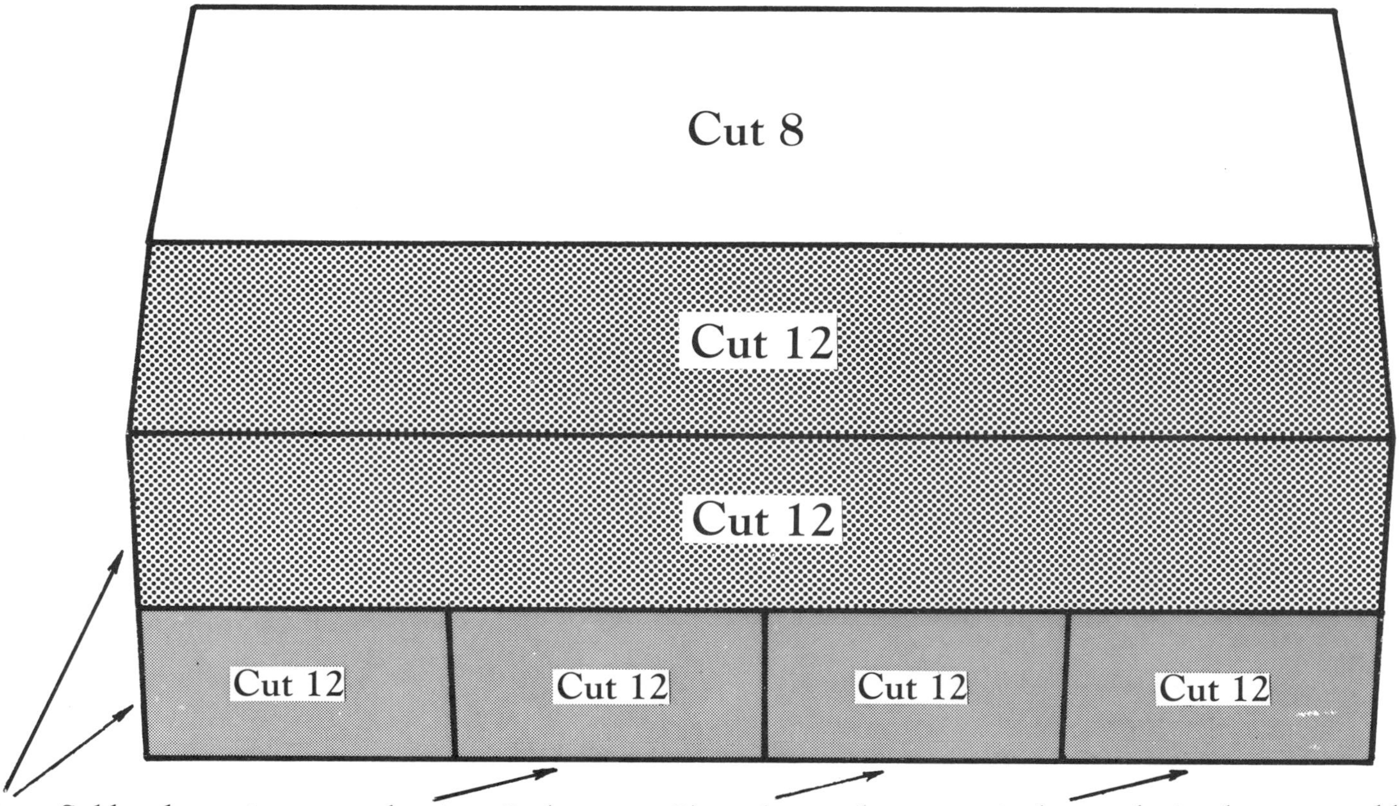

Cut 8

Cut 12

Cut 12

Cut 12   Cut 12   Cut 12   Cut 12

Note: Solder these pieces together in a jig (see page 7) and treat them as a single row during lamp assembly

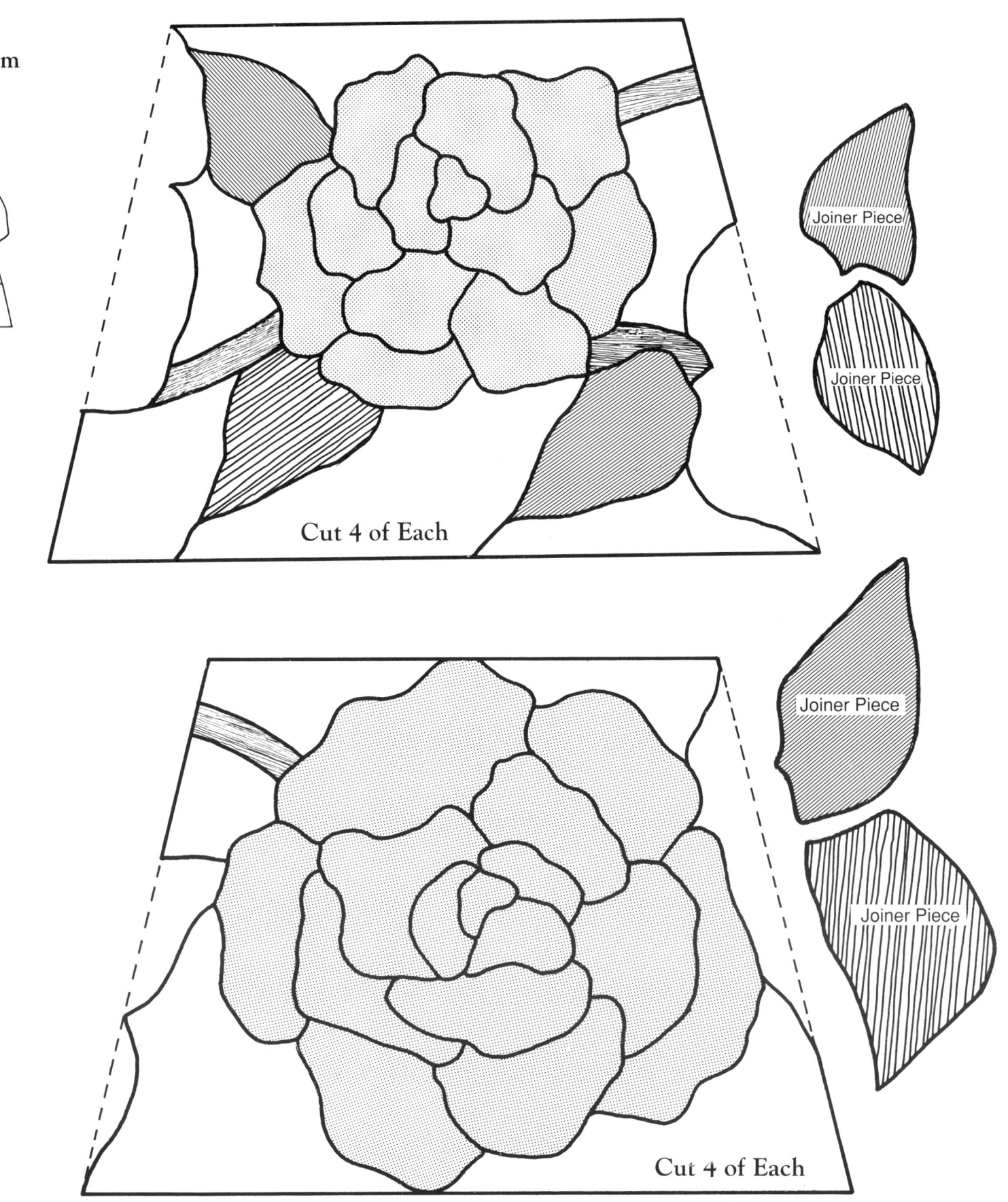

Project 16   OLD ROSE

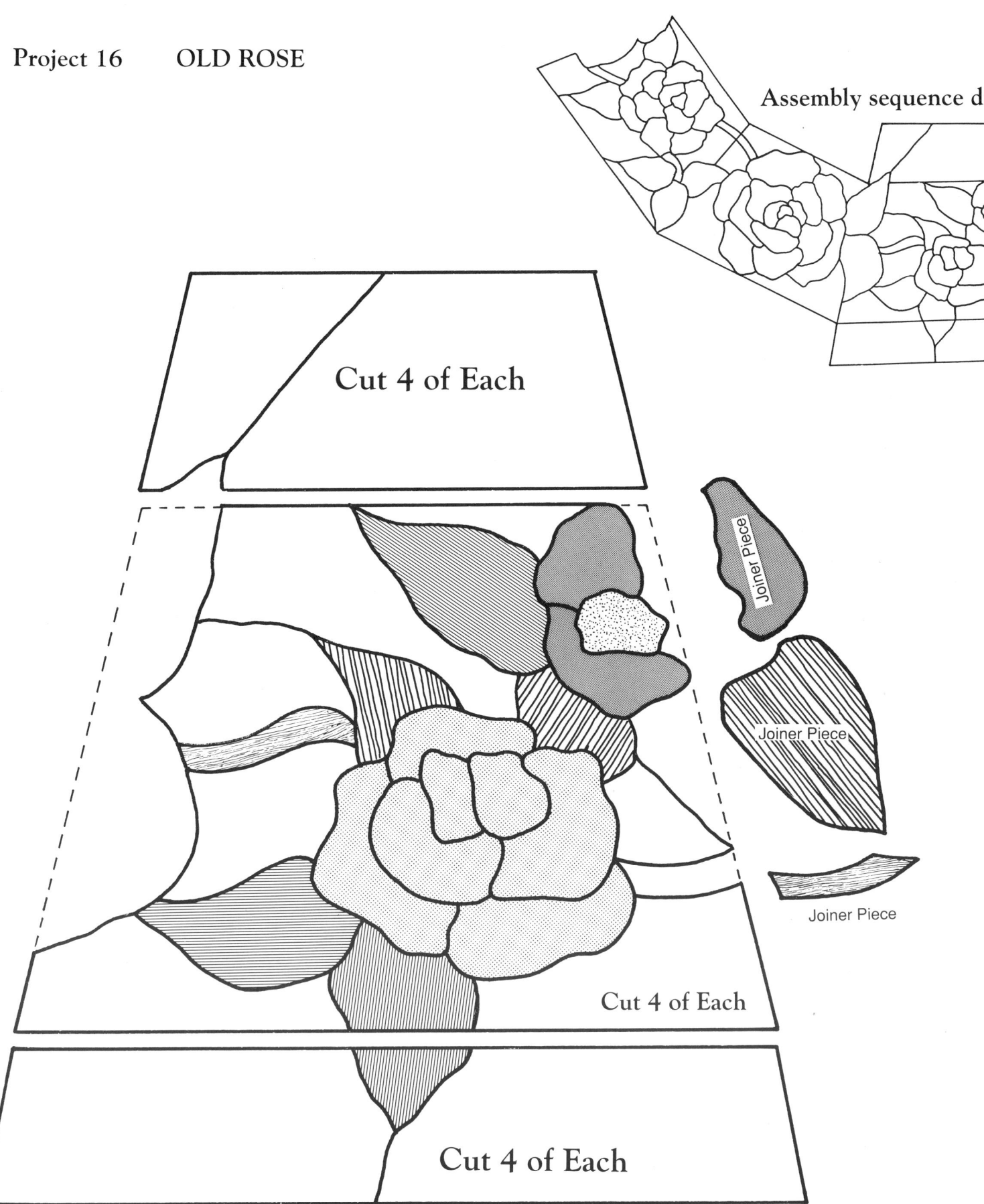

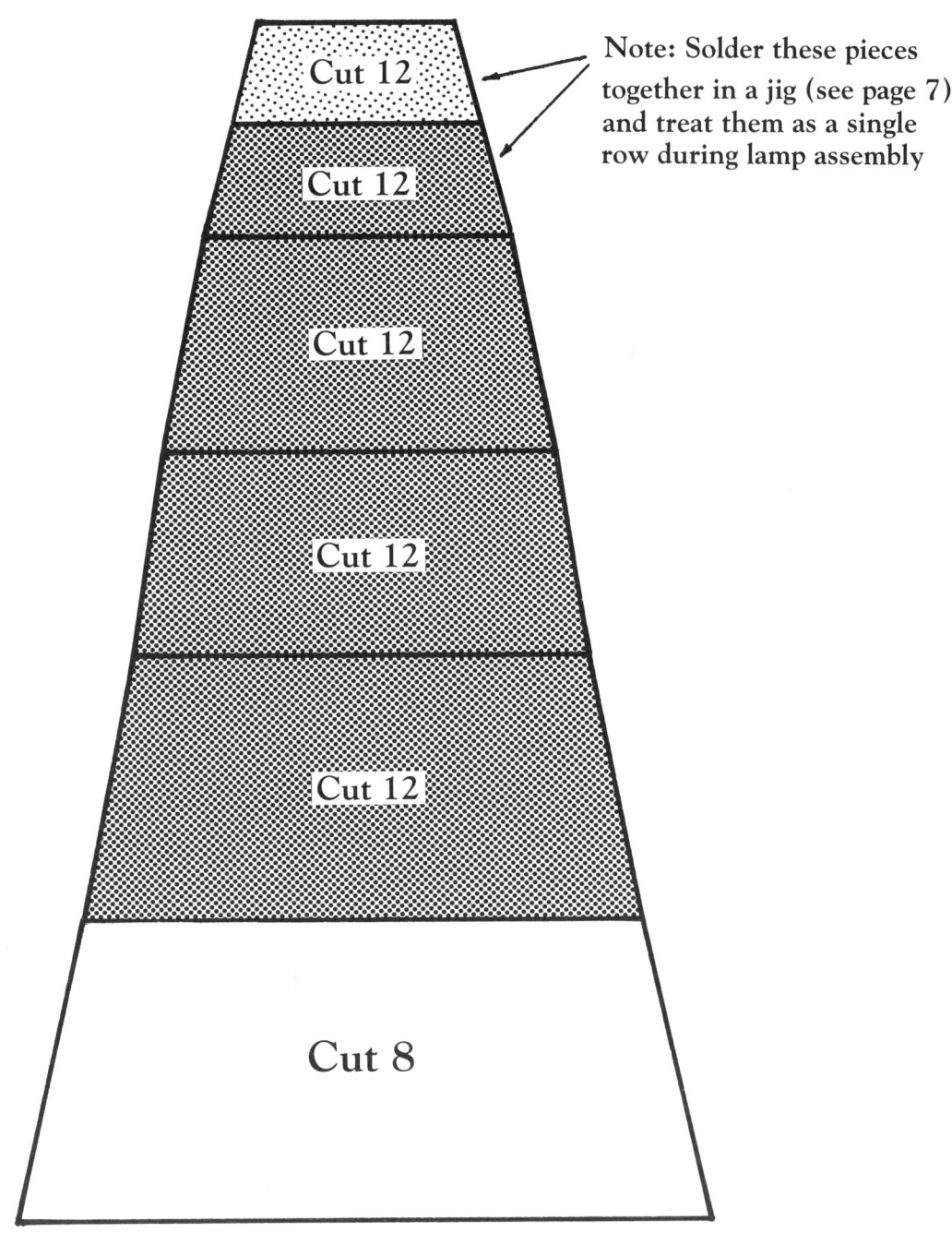

Project 12   DRAPERY

                            Cut 10 of Each

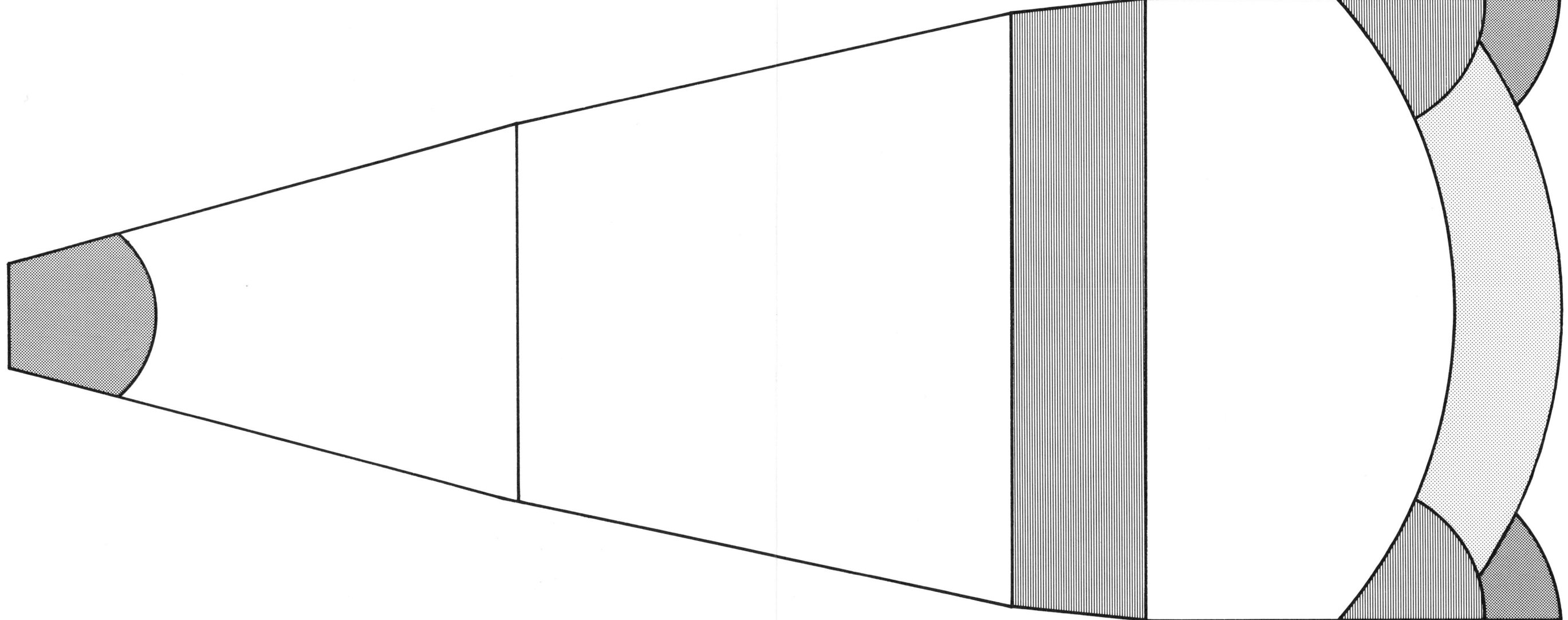

Project 13

LILY

Cut 6 of Each

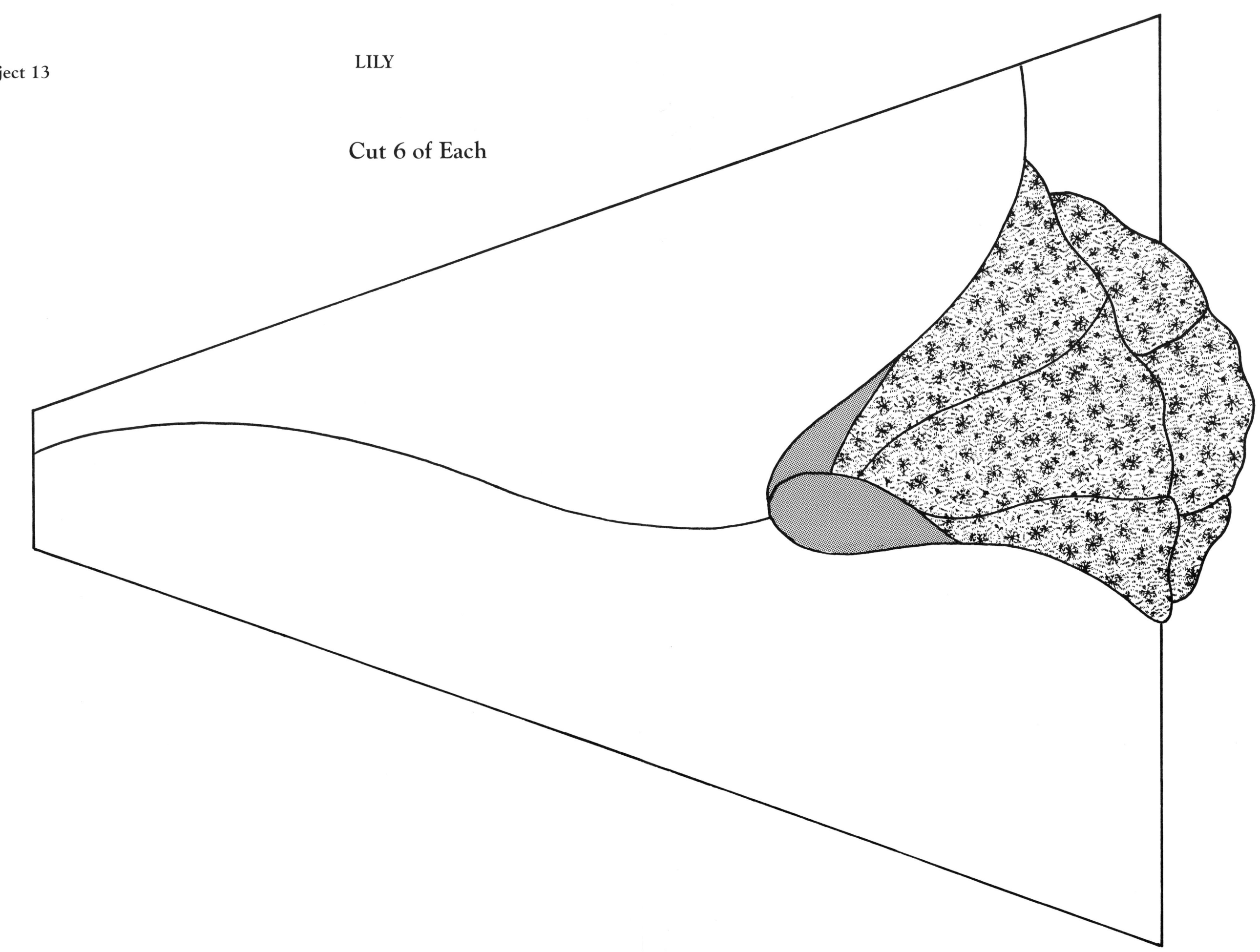

Project 10

BARCELONA CONE

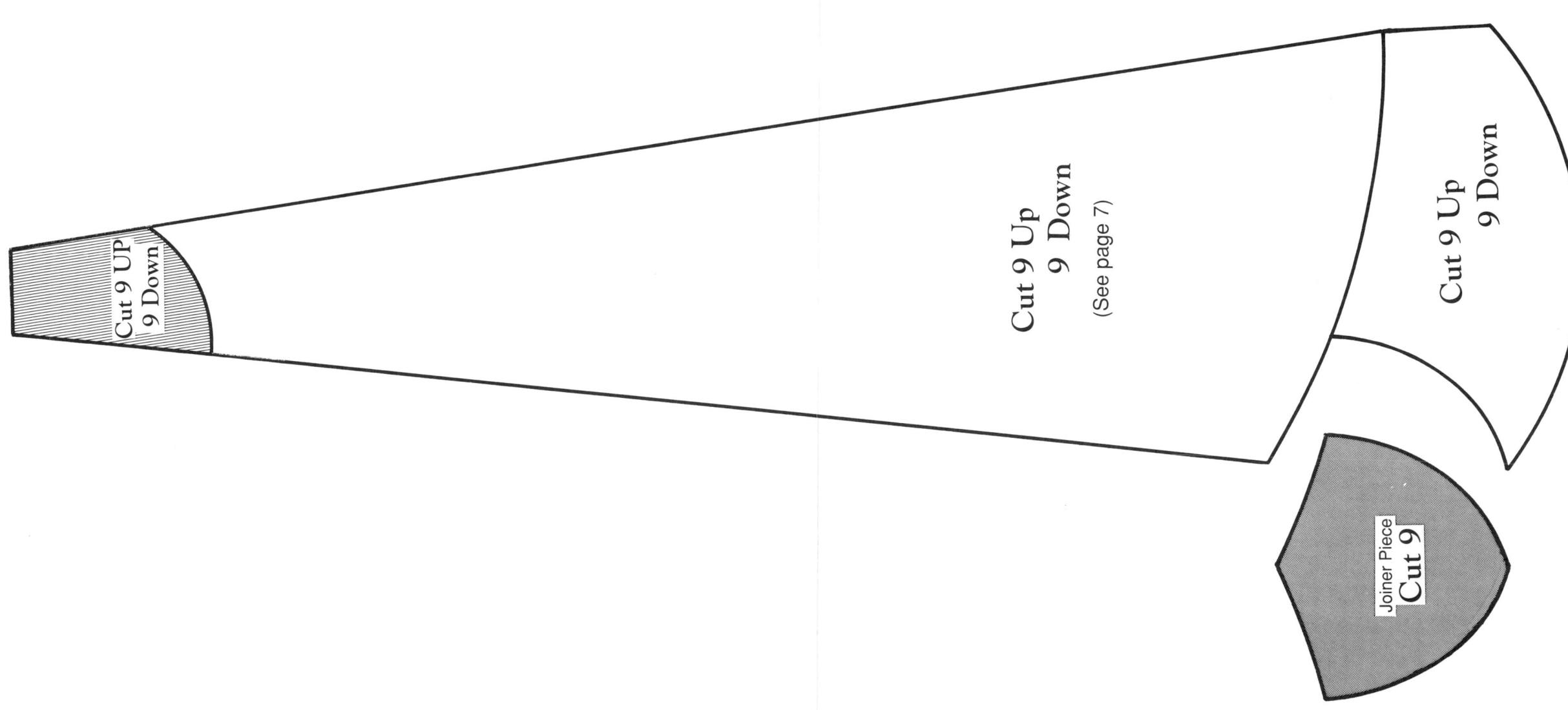

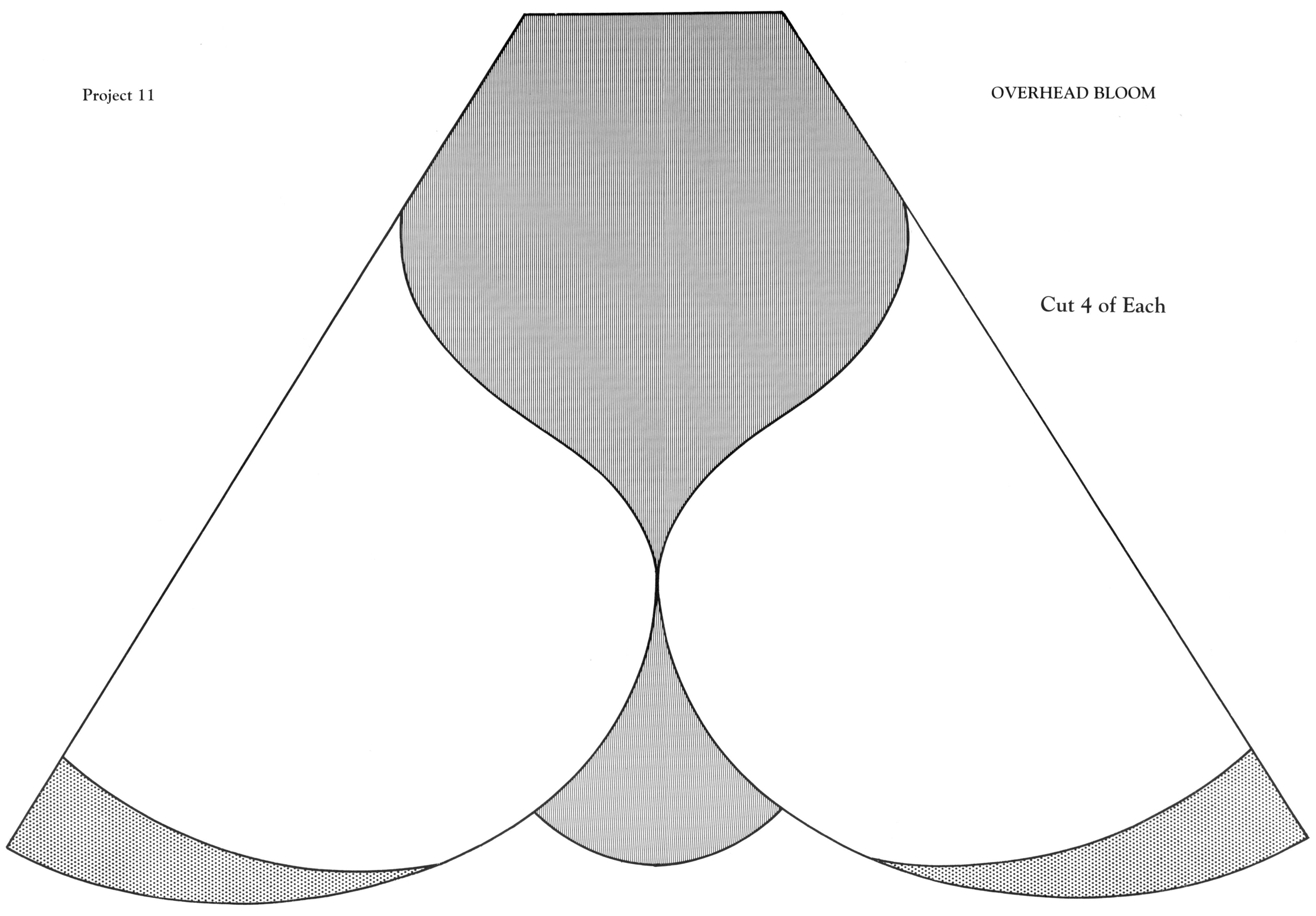

Project 14

TULIP BELL

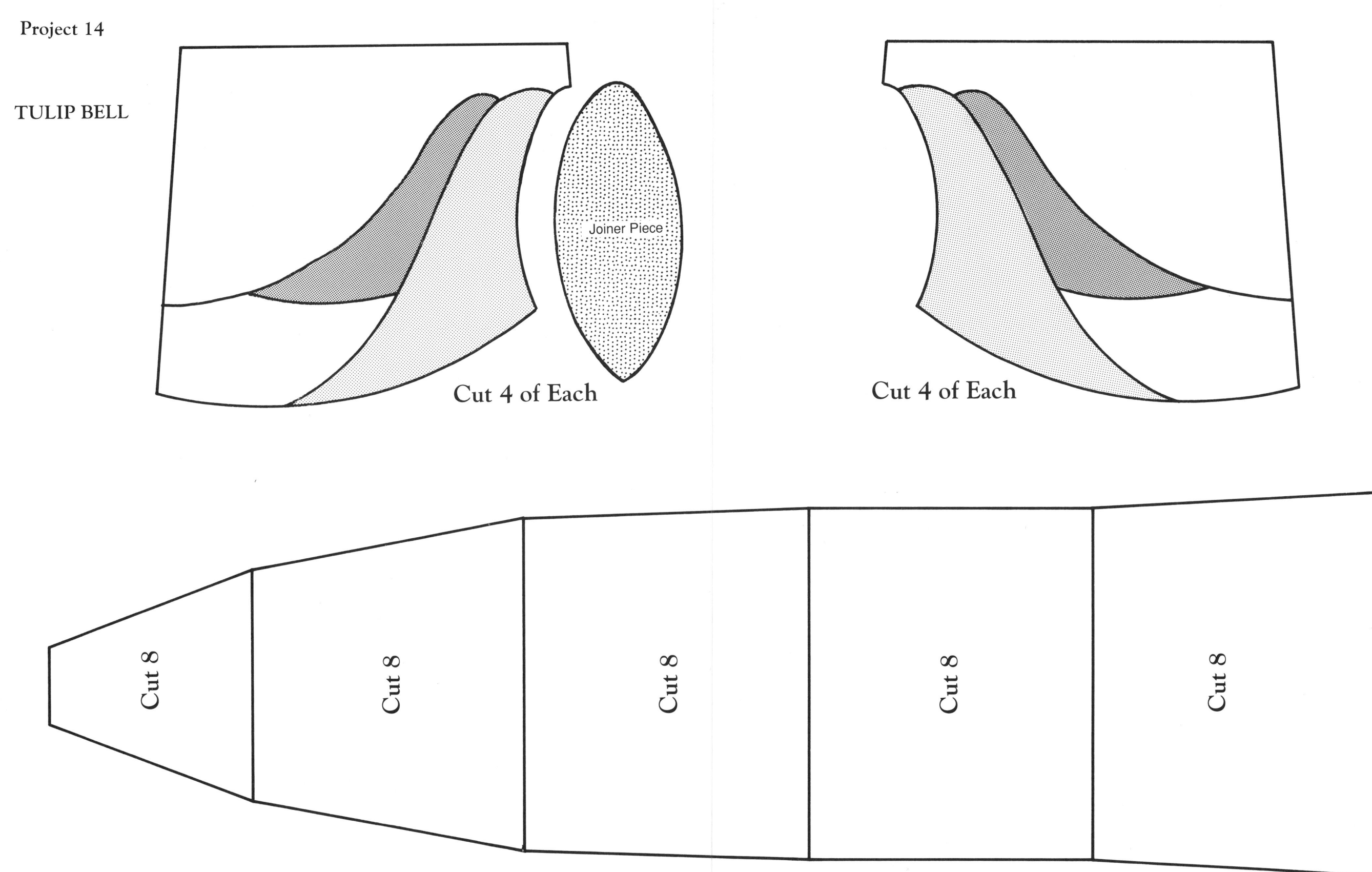

Cut 4 of Each

Joiner Piece

Cut 4 of Each

Cut 8 Cut 8 Cut 8 Cut 8 Cut 8

Project 15 RIDEAU

Cut 6 of Each

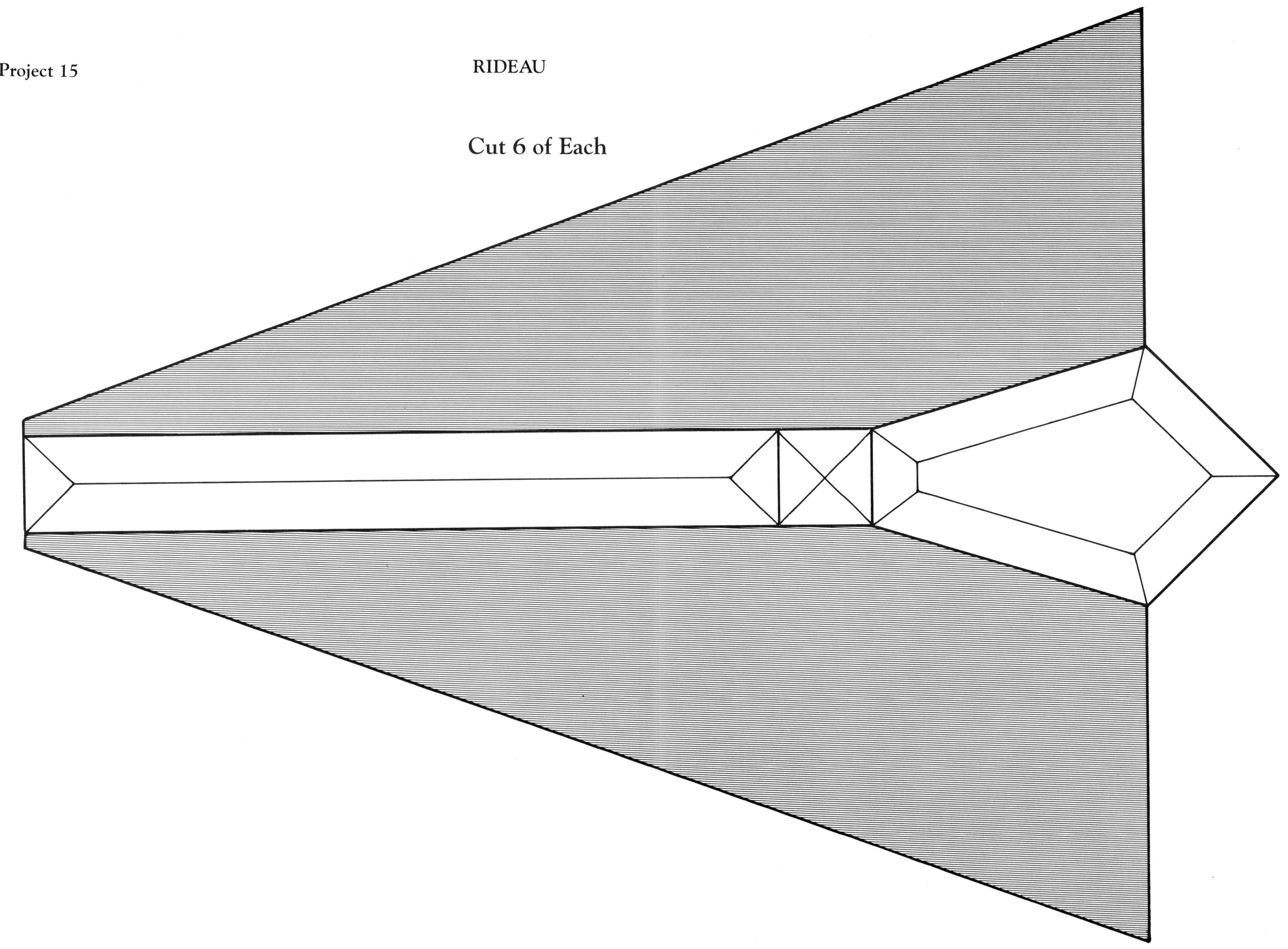

INTRODUCTION TO STAINED GLASS   70 pgs   17 Patterns   985041
This book is designed to be used as a do-it-yourself manual or to supplement an instructional course. It provides all the step-by-step information on tools, supplies and techniques necessary to learn on your own. Patterns are included for 17 projects ranging from sun catchers and windows to lampshades.

LAMPSHADE PATTERNS I   48 pgs   22 Patterns   985009
Full-size patterns for 22 shades ranging in diameter from 5" to 16". All are shown in color, matched with an appropriate lampbase. Included is an instruction guide with trade secrets to assist all crafters in lampshade assembly.

MORE LAMPSHADE PATTERNS II   28 pgs   11 Patterns   985050
Step-by-step instructions and full-size patterns for 11 large swag-style shades. The designs include six dining room lamps (16" to 22") a 15" x 27" pool table lamp and four (14" to 19") living room styles. All projects shown in full color.

DESIGNS FOR LAMPS by C. Knapp   48 pgs   18 Patterns   985068
An exciting collection of full-size patterns for 18 lampshades from 6" to 15" in diameter. These shades were designed primarily to be mounted on a lampbase and information to help match the base to shade is provided. Assembly instructions included.

LAMPWORKS   46 pgs   16 Patterns   985149
This book contains 16 full-size patterns by five different designers. Their designs include three inverted ceiling lampshades, four table-lamp styles and nine swag lamps. Three of the shades incorporate bevels and for a challenge there is an elaborate 24" diameter old rose dining room lamp. Assembly instructions included.

STAINED GLASS BOXES   68 pgs   34 Patterns   985017
A complete book of 34 patterns for the always popular glass box. The styles range from mini ring boxes to a storage box for audio cassettes. The simple assembly steps are fully explained and all boxes are shown in color.

TERRARIUMS & PLANTERS   68 pgs   30 Patterns   985025
This comprehensive book contains a wide range of designs for 30 plant containers. The step-by-step assembly instructions are accompanied by a helpful guide to selecting and caring for plants in terrariums. All planters are photographed in color.

WALL DECORATIONS   68 pgs   29 Patterns   985033
This detailed book contains 29 patterns for clocks, mirrors & picture frames. Projects include a 30" high granddaughter clock, 11", 22" & 29" oval mirrors, a pendulum schoolhouse clock and much more. All are shown in color with assembly instructions.

GLASS SENSATIONS   68 pgs   22 Patterns   985081
This book is a collection of 22 full-size patterns for a variety of birds, flowers and plants. With a realistic design style and careful attention to detail these patterns offer projects that may take a few hours to some that are major undertakings. All are shown in color with assembly instructions.

CLASSIC ALPHABETS by T. Martin   48 pgs   8 Patterns   985130
This book contains three complete alphabet styles and two numeral styles. There are 20 line drawings of project ideas for use in traditional stained glass or sandetching. The information section covers the use of letters, creating a full-size drawing, dividing the background and use of color.

BEVEL WINDOW DESIGNS   72 pgs   114 Drawings   985076
This book has 32 color photographs and over 100 detailed line drawings of beveled glass windows offering a broad range of styles including traditional, floral & birds, and landscapes. An instructional section explains methods for pattern enlarging, custom designing, framing and much more.

FLOWERS - Set 1   3 Full-size Window Patterns   by R. & J. Wardell   985101
- MAGNOLIA-   -20" X 28"
- IRIS-   -20 1/4 X 36 1/4"
- FLOWERS IN VASE-   -12" X 18"

FLAMINGO & FLOWERS - Set 2   3 Full-size Window Patterns   by R. & J. Wardell   985102
- FLAMINGO-   -25 1/4" X 36 1/2"
- FLORAL VALANCE-   -8" X 31"
- IRIS-   -10 1/4" X 31 1/4"

SPORT & LEISURE - Set 3   3 Full-size Window Patterns   by R. & J. Wardell   985103
- SAILBOAT-   -26" X 27"
- GOLFER-   -15 3/4" X 19 3/4"
- LARGEMOUTH BASS-   -12" X 20"

BIRDS, BIRDS, BIRDS - Set 4   5 Full-size Window Patterns   by L. Doran & B. McMillan   985104
- CANADA GOOSE-   -24" Diameter
- SEAGULL & RAINBOW-   -10" X 11 1/2"
- BLUEJAY-   -15" X 17"
- CARDINAL-   -15" X 17"
- SMALL CANADA GOOSE-   -7 1/2" Diameter

Published by:

Wardell PUBLICATIONS

P.O. Box 1501 Belleville, Ontario, Canada
K8N 5J2 • (613) 962-6409

Available from: (dealer stamp)

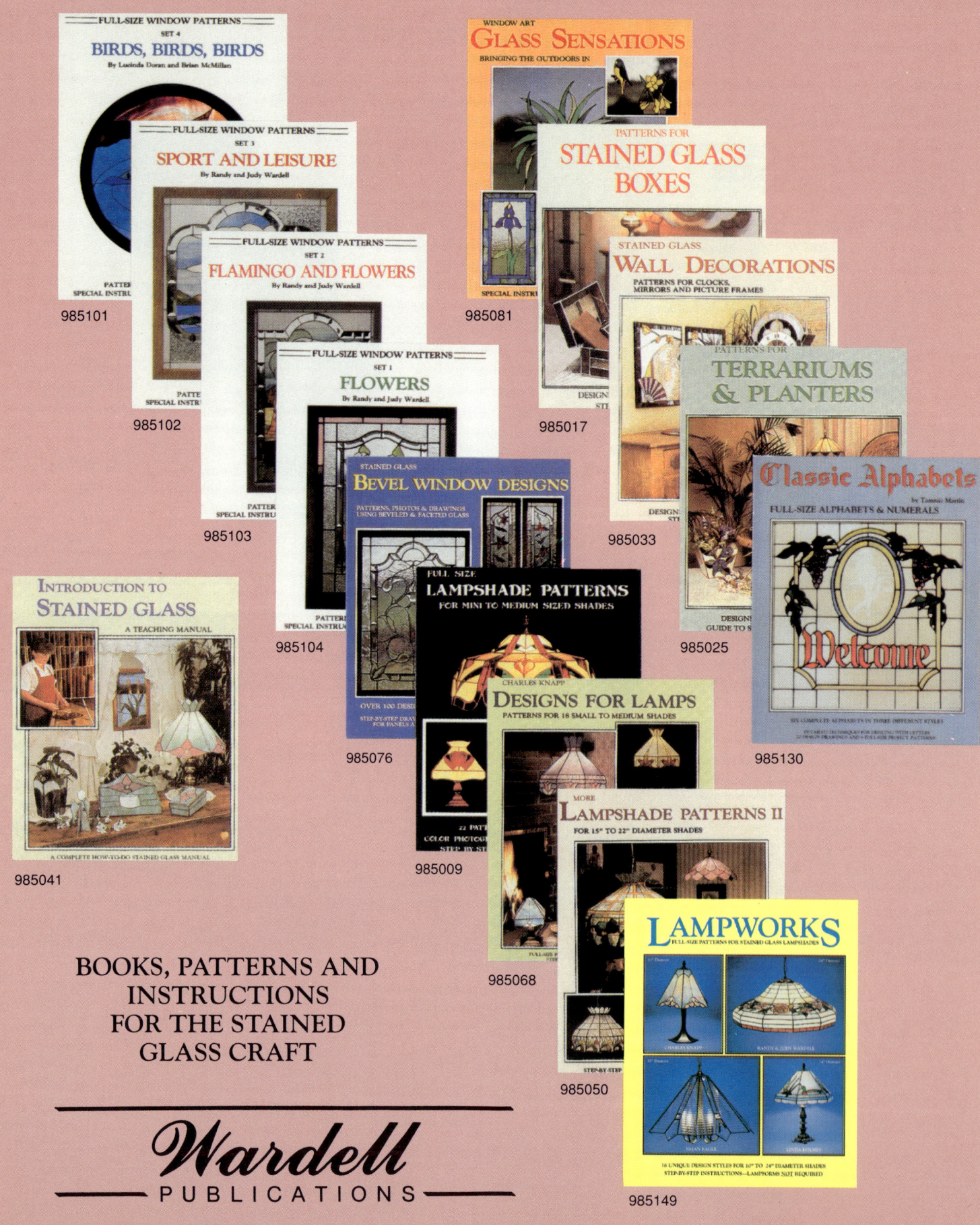